DID JESUS RISE FROM THE DEAD?

DID JESUS RISE FROM THE DEAD?

by

JAMES MARTIN

THE SAINT ANDREW PRESS
EDINBURGH

First published by United Society for Christian Literature 1956

Re-issued 1978 by
THE SAINT ANDREW PRESS
121 George Street, Edinburgh

© James Martin

ISBN 0 7152 0382 7

*The Scripture quotations in this book are from the
Revised Standard Version of the Bible*

Printed and bound in Great Britain by
T. & A. Constable Ltd, Edinburgh

PREFACE

A book on the resurrection is bound to be an interesting book because it deals with the central fact of the Christian faith. James Martin's book is a very worthwhile contribution to the literature on the resurrection. It is written simply in the sense that the ordinary reader can understand it, but it is written out of a background of scholarship which always shines through. It is written positively. It has the will to believe, not the will to disbelieve which is typical of so many modern theologians. It carefully adduces the evidence for the resurrection but it never suppresses attacks upon the resurrection and the questioning of the evidence. It is a notably fair book.

We have no doubt that this book will challenge the unbelief of the sceptic and will stimulate the belief of the believer. It is a book for all to read and there is no reader who will not benefit by reading it. We wish it every success in its new form.

WILLIAM BARCLAY

CONTENTS

INTRODUCTION

This book is an attempt to show that the historical evidence for the Resurrection of Jesus Christ is exceedingly strong—far stronger than many people, believers and unbelievers alike, are aware. Its argument is that the evidences are such as leave no reasonable doubt that Jesus of Nazareth, after He had been put to death by crucifixion, was raised from the dead and was seen alive by His disciples during the following forty days; and that this Resurrection meant more than the survival of His spirit, since it involved the raising of His body in such a manner that His grave was left empty.

No event in all history has greater importance than the Resurrection of Jesus, and there is none the truth of which matters so much. For, if the Resurrection be true, the Gospel of Christ is a real Gospel; if it be false, the Gospel falls to the ground. The apostle Paul, writing in the infancy of the Church, said this very thing: "If Christ has not been raised, then our preaching is in vain and your faith is in vain" (1 Cor. 15 : 14). The Resurrection is the keystone of the faith, and was at once the cause and the motive and the central affirmation of the apostolic preaching. One need only read the Acts of the Apostles to learn this.

Critics sometimes ask, "Why does the Church not

give up preaching the Resurrection of Jesus, which so many find a stumbling-block? Why is it not content to preach the simple Gospel?" The answer is that, if the Resurrection were abandoned, no Gospel would remain. That Christ was risen was the message that the believers of the New Testament period were concerned to make known. This was their Good News. They never for a moment imagined that the Resurrection was not vital to the Gospel, or that there could be a sufficient Gospel apart from the Resurrection. "For them," says A. M. Ramsey, "the Gospel without the Resurrection was not merely a Gospel without its final chapter; it was not a Gospel at all."[1]

It was an amazing message that the apostles released upon the world. C. E. M. Joad once said that, if he were allowed to interview any personage of the past, he would wish to speak with Jesus of Nazareth and put to Him "the most important question in the world: 'Did you or did you not rise from the dead?'" In thus describing the question Dr. Joad made no overstatement.

Let us, however, hasten to make plain that acceptance of the historical truth of the Resurrection is not the same as having faith in the Resurrection. A man is a Christian not by virtue of mere intellectual assent to any propositions, historical or otherwise, concerning Jesus—although the giving of such assent will often be the necessary preliminary—but by virtue of having that faith in the Risen Christ, which is both an act of his own will and the gift of God.

There is a story told of Blondin, the famous tight-rope walker, that on one occasion he had carried a

[1] *The Resurrection of Christ*, p. 7.

10

man across a tight-rope stretched perilously above an admiring crowd. In the forefront of the crowd was a boy, gazing at the feat in open-mouthed wonderment. Blondin noticed the lad and said to him, "Do you believe that I could carry you across that tight-rope?" The boy replied, "I am sure you could." "Well, then," said Blondin, "jump up and I will do so." But this was a different affair, and the boy declined the invitation.

This story roughly illustrates the difference that must be recognized between a conviction that the Resurrection took place and faith in the Risen Christ. Despite what he believed about Blondin's prowess, the boy was not prepared to trust his life into Blondin's keeping. Similarly, it is not enough to believe that Jesus has risen from the dead and is alive to-day. Faith involves taking a further step, the taking of which will depend on that belief but which will carry a man far beyond it, and mean the committing of himself in complete confidence to the living Christ.

CHAPTER ONE

WITH AN OPEN MIND

A century ago Dr. Thomas Arnold of Rugby, sometime Professor of History at Oxford, wrote these words: "I have been used for many years to study the history of other times, and to examine and weigh the evidence of those who have written about them; and I know of no fact in the history of mankind which is proved by better and fuller evidence of every sort, *to the understanding of a fair inquirer*, than the great sign that God has given us, that Christ died and rose again from the dead." [1]

The evidence for the Resurrection is, indeed, of tremendous strength. Why, then, do many people to-day doubt it and dispute it? Part, at least, of the explanation would appear to be that many have such a deep-rooted prejudice against belief in the Resurrection that their prejudice makes it extremely difficult for them to give the evidence a fair hearing. Dominated by the "modern mind", they find it well-nigh impossible to think of the Resurrection as a real possibility. Miracles, they are sure, do not happen, cannot happen, never did happen. Therefore the Resurrection cannot be true.

We do not suggest that all who refuse to accept the Resurrection of Jesus as a historical fact answer to this description. There are those who believe that

[1] *Sermon on the Sign of the Prophet Jonas.*

Jesus lives on to-day—in His influence in His followers and in the world generally—but do not believe in His Resurrection. And there are those who believe in a spiritual Resurrection of Jesus, and who honestly try to live their lives in fellowship with Him; but do not believe that He rose from the dead in such a way that His grave was left empty. We may reckon as deficient the Christian faith of such people, but they are in a different category from the sceptics. There are, too, many who accept the full Resurrection belief, but at times find doubts or questionings concerning it arising in their minds.

The type of sceptic, who summarily dismisses the Resurrection as untrue, often claims that it is his scientific outlook which causes him to do so. His approach is, in fact, not the scientific approach at all. The scientific method is to come to any given problem with as open a mind as possible, fairly and fully to consider the relevant evidence, and to proceed in the light of that evidence to reach conclusions. As things are, many people do not take the trouble to listen to the evidence, because of their conviction that the Resurrection is something in which it is impossible to believe. This is a great pity, since their basic assumption, that miracle is impossible, cannot be scientifically justified.

It may be well at this point to ask what we mean by the word "miracle". One dictionary definition is "an event or effect in the physical world deviating from the known laws of nature, or transcending our knowledge of those laws." For the Christian this is far too wide a definition; there are a great many such events or effects which he would not class as miracles, since that word, as he uses it, applies only to "events or effects" caused by the direct action of God in the world which He has made, and in which He still acts in loving care for His children. Miracles are the bringing about by God, in response to human need, and often in response to human prayers, of results which would not have come about otherwise, at least not in quite that way.

It is simply arbitrary to declare that miracles do not happen and cannot happen. Even science has no authority to make such a declaration. The most that science could do, were it so minded, would be to state that it had not yet encountered a proved case of miracle.

Nevertheless, there are some who say, "Whatever be the evidence for the Resurrection, we will not believe it, for we know that it is impossible." They may remind us of the little girl who was being taken through the multiplication table by her grandfather. "Six times six?" he asked her, and she replied triumphantly, "Thirty-six." "Nine times nine?" "Eighty-one." And then, "Thirteen times thirteen?" Whereupon the little girl turned on him scornfully, "There is no such thing." But the mere fact of any given thing never having come within the range of our personal experience is no ground for assuming that it is non-existent.

More than forty years ago, James Orr wrote these words: "Professor Huxley and J. S. Mill are probably as good authorities on science as most, and both tell us that there is no scientific impossibility in miracle—it is purely and solely a question of evidence."[1] And this was when science was much more self-confident than the best scientists are to-day.

[1] *The Resurrection of Jesus*, p. 50.

Most scientists to-day would readily admit that miracle is not a scientific impossibility.

Miracle indeed could rightly be deemed impossible only if it could be proved that God did not exist. If a man believes that God exists, there is for him no reasonable difficulty in believing that miracles may happen. And, even where a man has no real belief in God's existence, so long as he admits the *possibility* of God's existence—so long, that is, as he is unable to prove that God does not exist—he must admit also the possibility of miracle. Since, therefore, the existence of God cannot be *disproved* (though it can be doubted), the possibility of miracle can never wholly be ruled out. And so, not only for the theist but for the atheist also, the only legitimate question concerning the historical truth of any alleged miracle (and concerning the Resurrection in particular) is this—"Is the evidence strong enough to justify belief in it?"

Not that all, or even most, of those who are sceptical about the Resurrection consciously shut their minds to the possibility of its being true. Many people who would like to believe are unable to shake themselves free of the conviction that such a thing could not be. But the fact is that for many the main obstacle to belief in the Resurrection is the presence in their minds of a stubborn prejudice against its supranormal character. Nevertheless, the evidence, if given a chance, may well overcome this prejudice. The experience of Frank Morison, the author of *Who Moved the Stone?* is relevant here. He tells us that, when he first purposed to write a book on the Resurrection, it was a sceptical treatment that he had in mind, for he was one who considered that the miraculous did not happen. But, when he investigated the evidence, he found it so persuasive in spite of his sceptical approach that instead of the book originally intended he wrote one defending the truth of the Resurrection.

The Resurrection, of course, cannot be "proved" in the manner of a mathematical demonstration or a laboratory experiment. All that we can do—which indeed, is all that can be done in relation to any fact of history—is to point out that there is a convergence of historical probabilities, which places the historicity of the Resurrection beyond all reasonable doubt. A. M. Ramsey says that what can be shown is that "certain historical facts are unaccountable apart from the Resurrection, and that different lines of historical testimony so converge as to point to the Resurrection with overwhelming probability" [1]—in much the same way as "if half a dozen signposts, with the name of the same village painted on them, all point one way, then sincerity in regard to the evidence compels belief that the village exists, even though we have never been there". [2] Recognizing this, it is still true to say that the historical evidence for the Resurrection, as constituted by this convergence of probabilities, is overwhelming, and is, indeed, far stronger than the evidence for many other events of history which everyone accepts unhesitatingly as true. That scepticism persists is due largely, not to any deficiencies in the evidence, but to the extraordinary character of the event itself.

[1] *The Resurrection of Christ*, p. 36.
[2] L. Weatherhead, *The Resurrection and the Life*, p. 18.

CHAPTER TWO

THE DOCUMENTS

All the relevant documentary evidence concerning the Resurrection is contained in the New Testament; and the message of the Lord's rising from the dead underlies its every page. "The whole New Testament literature is radiant with the light of the Resurrection." [1]

We take account particularly of the letters of Paul, Peter's speeches in Acts, and the four Gospels, for their witness is the clearest and the most valuable for our purpose.

Paul's Letters. In the course of his missionary travels, and as a result of his intimate relationship with many of the Churches, Paul must have written a great many letters, dealing with matters of the faith, of Church order and of Christian doctrine. Some of these survived and stand now in the New Testament Canon. Written as they were within the four decades following the Death and Resurrection of Jesus, and embodying at times material the origin of which dates back much earlier than the epistle which contains it, they provide priceless testimony to the belief of the early Church concerning the Resurrection.

The most important passage is 1 Corinthians 15 : 3–8. It runs: "For I delivered to you as of first importance what I also received, that Christ died for

[1] A. M. Hunter, *Life and Words of Jesus,* p. 123.

18

our sins in accordance with the scriptures, that he was buried, that he was raised on the third day in accordance with the scriptures, and that he appeared to Cephas, then to the twelve. Then he appeared to more than five hundred brethren at one time, most of whom are still alive, though some have fallen asleep. Then he appeared to James, then to all the apostles. Last of all, as to one untimely born, he appeared also to me."

Paul, writing this letter about A.D. 55, reminds his readers of how he had preached the Gospel to them in person (15 : 1). Then he says, "I delivered to you as of first importance what I also received". His preaching to the Corinthians had been, in the first instance, the relaying of a message, which was not his own invention nor his own theorizing, but which had been *given* to him—given him by the Church through one or more of its representatives—and given presumably at the time of his conversion. Now Paul's conversion occurred no later than A.D. 35. That is to say, the message of the Lord's Resurrection, which came to him with the authority of the Church at his conversion and which he later passed on to the Corinthians and of which he now gives reminder, goes back to a point not more than six years after the first Easter.

Moreover, the passage which then follows (15 : 3–7) reads as if Paul were quoting a familiar formula, possibly one that was in general use in that first decade for the instruction of converts or as a sort of creed. Paul has added to the formula a reference to his own vision of the Risen Lord (15 : 8); but the indications are that he is here giving to his readers not merely a reminder that, at the time of his conversion, the Church had already a fixed Resurrection tradition, but an actual formula embodying the Church's belief concerning the Resurrection, which may well have come into being at an early period and, at latest, before Paul's first visit to Corinth.

Peter's Speeches in Acts. Acts was almost certainly written by Luke, author also of the Gospel that bears his name. He was a careful and, viewed in the light of the standards of that day, a remarkably accurate historian. Tested even against the standards of our own day, Luke's reliability has been confirmed by modern research and investigation. He was not himself, as it appears, a hearer of these first Christian sermons, but he must have had several sources of information which he would sift and check to the best of his considerable ability (just as he did when writing his Gospel, Luke 1 : 1–4). We cannot regard the records of Peter's speeches in the Acts as verbatim reports of what Peter said on any given occasion, but we may feel confident that they are an accurate representation of the gist of what he said.

The passages which thus give summaries of some of Peter's earliest public utterances are Acts 1 : 16–22; Acts 2 : 14–40; Acts 3 : 12–26; Acts 4 : 9–12; Acts 10 : 34–43. In each of them the same note is dominant and recurring, that the Lord is risen.

The Gospels. The four Gospels are not biographies of Jesus in anything approaching the modern meaning of biography. They do not seek to be exhaustive accounts of the life of Jesus, but are simply a few carefully selected reminiscences of that life, chosen from a vast reserve of material. But although the Gospels are very short books, and although limitations of space meant that the writers had to leave out much more than they were able to include, each devotes a large proportion of his space to the story of the Death and Resurrection of Jesus. The writers were men of different qualities and different temperaments, writing in different places and from different points of view; this being so, their combined testimony to the Resurrection, and their allotting of so much of their limited space to it, are surely most significant. They show that the Resurrection of Jesus was central to the Church's faith from the very beginning.

But, in order to assess rightly the value of the documentary evidence, it will be well to consider first how the Gospels came to be written.

There were three stages in the process that brought the Gospels into being—the Stage of Happening, the Stage of Speech and the Stage of Writing. These stages were not rigidly exclusive but were, none the less, quite distinct.

i. The Stage of Happening. For about three years Jesus moved up and down Palestine, preaching the way of God and performing many works of love and mercy. Then he journeyed to Jerusalem for what proved to be His last visit to that city. There He was arrested, condemned and crucified. The sequel, so His followers asserted, was that He was raised from the dead and appeared to them many times, before His visible presence was finally withdrawn from them.

ii. The Stage of Speech. Then followed what is more commonly known as the period of oral tradition, during which the story of Jesus was preserved and passed on mainly by word of mouth.

The river of oral reminiscence flowed along two

21

main channels—missionary preaching, and the worship of the Christian assemblies. The missionary preaching began almost at once. Transformed and exultant, the Christians began to tell to all who would listen their good news of Him whom they believed to be Saviour and Lord. From the very beginning also, side by side with the missionary preaching, were the meetings of the Christians for worship. At these weekly assemblies, part of the service was devoted to hearing someone of authority speak about the Lord. And so the stories of Jesus were told and retold.

Foremost among these stories and by far the most frequently narrated was the story of Jesus' Death and Resurrection. This *was* the Gospel, the Good News—that Jesus of Nazareth, who had been crucified, had triumphed over death.

The story of the Lord's Death and Resurrection constituted the main stream in the river of oral tradition. But it was not the only stream. Another was the recollection of things Jesus had said and done. It was important that these also should be remembered, for the corollary of having faith in Jesus the Saviour was that one must live in accordance with the example and the command of Christ the King.

Some stories would appeal more than others to a certain community. The favourite stories would come to be told more and more often, while others would drop gradually out of the picture, and so the tradition of that particular community would be formed. The result was that, while the main body of oral tradition was the same everywhere, no two districts had exactly the same collection of reminiscences. The Church at Jerusalem, for instance, would contain in its tradition some items that the Church at Caesarea did not, and *vice versa*; and some of the stories common to both would be told in different ways in each.

Soon these separate oral traditions began to assume unchanging forms, as constant repetition rendered them more or less fixed in each Church and district; and so the oral tradition of each area became a thing of individuality, basically the same as those of other areas but recognizably distinct from them.

iii. The Stage of Writing. The opening verses of Luke's Gospel (Luke 1 : 1–4) make it plain that earlier than our four Gospels were other writings, probably of a more fragmentary and less systematic kind, none of which has survived. But, on the whole, during the first generation of the Christian Church, there was little activity in the way of writing down the Gospel tradition. It was only as the first generation of Christians began to thin, and, one after another, the voices of the eyewitnesses became still, that the need was felt to preserve the sacred story in more definite and more permanent form.

When the Stage of Writing arrived, those who took upon themselves the task of compiling written records found a mass of material ready to hand. The evangelists took this material, both oral and written, examined and sifted it, made their selections and wrote the short books which the Church has preserved down to our day in its Canon of Scripture.

Mark came first, probably between A.D. 60 and A.D. 65, perhaps earlier, and is based almost certainly on the recollections of Peter. Matthew, published probably between A.D. 80 and A.D. 85, may have been

23

based on diary notes of the apostle Matthew but used other sources as well. Luke, which was written about the same time as Matthew, is the work of a remarkably careful historian and used many sources, as its first four verses declare. John, perhaps between A.D. 95 and A.D. 100, may not have been written by the apostle himself but, if not, is probably the work of one of his disciples.

A reader who has grasped the manner in which the original eyewitness testimonies were preserved down the years, until a selection of their content was enshrined in the written Gospels, may well feel that we can accept these Gospels as substantially accurate transcriptions of the original stories. But we underline that thesis by taking up two questions:

1. Why was it so long after the events that the Gospels came to be written? It may seem strange that some 30 or 35 years should elapse before the appearance of the first Gospel. But several things should be borne in mind:

(*a*) We cannot assume that nothing was put into written form before Mark came on the scene. In all likelihood, several more fragmentary accounts of Jesus' teaching and works would have been written in the earlier period, although none of these, unfortunately, has survived independently. Some, however, would probably be used as sources, and thus part of their content may have been preserved in one or more of the four Gospels.

(*b*) The Christians of the first generation believed that the end of the world was very near; and to them, therefore, the writing of books would seem largely irrelevant and unnecessary.

(*c*) Allied to this was the intense missionary zeal

24

and activity which characterized the Christians of the early period. They were so busy evangelizing the world that there was little time for sitting down and writing books.

(d) The main reason, however, was that, during the first generation or so, the Christians felt neither need nor desire for written records. The Jews had been accustomed, for many generations, to pass on their history and their religious and social teaching by word of mouth, and regarded oral tradition as superior to the written word. The early Christians, Jewish in origin and background, shared this outlook. So long, therefore, as eyewitnesses survived, little room and little welcome existed for the more impersonal written record.

2. Can we be confident that the tradition was perpetuated accurately through the Stage of Speech to the Stage of Writing? Those who are accustomed to getting everything from books may feel it probable that, since the period of oral transmission was so long, the ultimate written form would deviate considerably from what had been originally told. Several things need to be said:

(a) The accuracy of verbal transmission on the part of the Jews was remarkable. The Jews mostly learned and taught by word of mouth. Their very word for instruction, *Mishnah*, means literally "repetition", and at once suggests that learning by heart which was the actual custom. From the beginning they showed great natural aptitude for it, and this, allied to long practice, produced memories of remarkable accuracy. Exactly the same is true in India and in other countries, where the training of the verbal memory is regarded as of great importance.

(*b*) The preservation of the oral tradition was never the concern of only a picked minority among the Christians. From the beginning this tradition was the property of the whole Church, and the whole Church was its guardian. We may be sure that, had any important deviation from the original ever occurred, at once many voices would have been raised in protest, and correction would have been demanded and obtained.

(*c*) But not only did every member of the Christian community have a part in maintaining the accuracy of its tradition; amongst that community were actual eyewitnesses, a fact of great significance. Some people seem to imagine that, after the initial telling of the story, every eyewitness immediately and for ever withdrew from the whole affair. The fact is that, right up to the beginning of the stage of writing and well on into it, there were in the Church surviving eyewitnesses, whose oversight of the tradition must have been sufficient to ensure substantial accuracy in its transmission.

Let us try to illustrate. There is a game, familiar to many readers, in which a message is passed verbally from one end of a line of people to the other. The players are strung across the room, and the starter whispers the message to the first person. That person, in turn, whispers the message—or what he has understood it to be—to his neighbour. At the end, it is frequently found that the message is most strangely distorted from its original form.

But it was not quite like this with the transmission of the Gospel tradition. Imagine that the room in which the game is played is one in which people are coming and going continually. At the beginning of the proceedings, someone narrates to the rest of the company an event that he and some companions, with him in the room now, had witnessed only that afternoon. Thereafter, the story is continuously told and retold by the first narrator and by others, and all the time there are arrivals and departures. This more closely resembles the circumstances under which the oral tradition was transmitted.

Imagine that there are several rooms, not merely one, with free passage between them, and that the same story is told in each, but by a different eyewitness; and that as the evening wears on, more and more people begin to write down parts of the story; and, finally, that, at the evening's close, each of four people who, if not present from the start, have, at least, been present for some considerable time, writes down, with others assisting him, a systematic version of the story. This gives a rough picture of what took place, as the Gospel tradition passed through the Stage of Speech and into the Stage of Writing.

(d) There is yet another feature in the Gospel narratives which strongly suggests that there can have been remarkably little tampering with the original stories. This is the presence of a considerable number of "awkward" items, sayings and references which were liable to cause difficulty or invite criticism, and which would certainly have been changed or eliminated had there been any substantial alteration or tidying up of the narratives.

Their presence is evidence that the Church, the custodian of the eyewitness accounts, showed respect for the facts, even when the facts were uncongenial. For instance, practically from the beginning, the Christians worshipped Jesus as God; yet we find it

27

recorded that Jesus cried from the Cross, "My God, my God, why hast thou forsaken me?" (Mark 15 : 34). Again, on not a few occasions, we find some uncomplimentary reference to one or other of the disciples, or a stark revelation of obtuseness or weakness or sin on their part. The presence of these things cannot be explained, unless the narratives which contain them have maintained remarkable fidelity to the truth. Had the narratives suffered serious modification in the process of transmission, the awkward items would have been the first to disappear.

CHAPTER THREE

THE TESTIMONY OF THE DOCUMENTS

We have chosen to confine our consideration of the written evidence to six New Testament writers, Matthew, Mark, Luke, John, Paul, Peter. What are we to make of their witness?

Theirs is striking testimony. Here are six men, bearing separate and independent[1] witness; all agree in affirming that Jesus had been raised from the dead. What is more, they are men of different temperaments; they are men who write at different times and in different places; they are men who have a right to speak, since all, in their various ways, have close associations with the early days of Christianity; they are men, indeed, who are either themselves eye-witnesses or have derived their information from those who were; and are, therefore, in a position to ascertain whether what they chronicle is indeed an accurate report of what took place. None of them, of course, had seen the actual Resurrection—no one had—but is it not most compelling that all six, in

[1] Objection may be taken to my use of the word "independent" here, in view of the fact that Matthew and Luke both made extensive use of Mark. Some would say, therefore, that the witness of the Synoptic Gospels is not threefold but one; and that, in the documents under review, we have not six witnesses but four. Nevertheless, it seems to me correct to regard our witnesses as six. For Matthew and Luke are independent witnesses in the sense that matters here, in the sense that, even though each used Mark as a reference book, each gives his own independent affirmation of the truth of what he writes.

their various ways and with their differing details, are at one in affirming that Jesus was raised? At any rate, the sceptic is not entitled simply to brush this testimony aside.

Some argue that no credence can be allowed to documents written so long after the events. This objection has already been met, and a few supplementary words will be sufficient here. The earliest of the Gospels was perhaps not written before A.D. 60; but, on the other hand, the latest was written before the end of the century. One of the most important writings we have considered, Paul's first Epistle to the Corinthians, was written about A.D. 55, less than thirty years after the first Easter, while another of Paul's letters, that to the Galatians, was probably written as early as A.D. 48. Men with intimate knowledge of important happenings, writing down their story twenty, thirty, even sixty years afterwards may be somewhat hazy about details, but will be in no doubt as to the main outline.[1] And our six writers were in no doubt that Jesus had risen.

Furthermore, what we have here is even more than the testimony of six witnesses. Behind their testimony lies the testimony of all the apostles and, indeed, of all the Church. These six men were not originating, they were transmitting, and the Resurrection belief that they affirmed was not just what they believed. It was what the Church believed, and what the Church had believed from the beginning.

Sometimes the sceptic argues that it is a suspicious

[1] One friend, who read this book in typescript, wrote: "It is now 52 years since I witnessed at close hand the great conflagration which destroyed the whole centre of the city of Baltimore in 1904. I was a boy at the time but every event of that conflagration and my contact with it is etched on my memory."

circumstance that all the early written evidence for the Resurrection is provided by people who believed in it. But it would have been remarkable had it been otherwise. In the earliest years no one except those who believed in it would have any occasion to write about the Resurrection, and there was no reason why any non-Christian writer of that time should refer to the small sect of the followers of Jesus. A parallel to this may be found in the fact that in the index to the fourteen volumes of the *Cambridge Modern History* there is only one reference to "missions", which are, nevertheless, by no means a negligible feature of recent times.

The sceptic may press his objection further and argue that, since the documents were written by Christians, they may be discounted as being biased witness. This is rather naïve. The Christian authorship of the documents does not alter the fact that they provide us with six separate testimonies to the Resurrection.

However, the strength of the evidence may best be felt by considering how strong it remains when reduced to its weakest state. Even when all the documentary evidence has been placed under the deepest suspicion, one thing remains absolutely certain—that from the beginning of the Church's life Christians believed that Jesus had risen from the dead. This is granted on all sides. It follows that, if the belief was not based on fact, there must be some other explanation of its origin.

But there are only three possible alternatives. One is that the first Christians perpetrated a gigantic fraud; the second is that, though sincere, they were the victims of delusion; the third, that the stories of the Resurrection came into being through the influence of similar resurrection-stories that were current in the non-Christian world of the time.

Was it Fraud? The suggestion that belief in the Resurrection was a falsehood successfully propagated by the first disciples must be prepared to meet a number of very serious objections.

In the first place the character of the Master they followed and of the moral principles that He had taught would seem to rule it out. Obedience to Him involved them in the obligation to be honest and truthful in all their dealings, and it is scarcely credible that they could have set about founding His Church on a deliberate lie.

Nor is it credible that a sheer invention on their part should have produced the results it did. Could they have been so invincibly enthusiastic concerning it, had the Easter story been something they had themselves made up? And how could a fabrication of their own have changed them, as they undoubtedly were changed, into men of new moral stature?

It is not even very credible that they could have carried out such a fraud with such astounding success. Was there any one of them, for instance, capable of the brilliant piece of organization that must have been involved? Peter is the most likely candidate for the job, but scarcely appears to have had the necessary qualifications. Not only so; but is it at all likely that the Resurrection preaching would have won so many converts in the beginning, if it had been based on a lie, which must in those earliest times have been very open to exposure? And to all this must be added the remarkable fact that apparently, during the years and during the suffering that followed, not one of those "in the know" ever gave away a hint that a fraud had been perpetrated.

Was it Delusion? This point will be dealt with more fully in chapters 5 and 6. At this point we simply pose two questions. First, had the Resurrection belief been the outcome of delusion, is it likely that so many different people as were involved at the beginning could have been individually and thoroughly convinced? Second, even assuming that Jesus' followers were casually and uncritically credulous of the Resurrection, is it not certain that those who were hostile to the belief would speedily have exposed it for the error that it was?

Was it Legend? A third suggestion has been made to the effect that the Resurrection story may be explained in terms of myths or legends of dying and rising gods that were current in the religious world of the time.

The argument usually runs something like this: Since legends of dying and rising gods were prevalent in the Mediterranean world, there would be a natural tendency for Christians to produce a similar legend of their own concerning the Founder of their religion. And so, in process of time, there crept into the story of Jesus the belief that He had risen from the dead. The argument may seem somewhat attractive, but the facts are against it.

For one thing, there was neither time nor opportunity for the Resurrection belief to have been a legendary development. Legend requires time for its growth. It does not spring up overnight like a mushroom. But the story of the Resurrection came into being simultaneously with the Church itself.

If events had run a different course; if, say, Jesus had been crucified, no word of Resurrection had been heard for a lapse of years, and then the story began to circulate that He had risen, one might have been entitled to suspect the influence of legend. But in actual fact the Resurrection belief came into being hard on the heels of the Crucifixion, and the message of the Resurrection was being publicly proclaimed no more than fifty days later. There was no room here for the intrusion of legend.

What is more, there is no evidence at all that the first Christians moved in an environment in which the Greek and Mediterranean legends were generally known. Some of them, no doubt, had contacts with Greek culture; but the background of most of them was predominantly, if not exclusively, Jewish; and the influences to which their thinking was exposed were those of orthodox Judaism and the Old Testament in particular. Such influences would incline them against, rather than·in favour of, the legends of resurrection.

Strongest argument of all, there is in fact not a single instance that is analogous with the Resurrection of Jesus. It is true that there were numerous legends of dying and rising gods in the Hellenistic world. But these all belonged without any doubt to the realm of mythology—legends that were known and accepted as such, and unlikely ever to be regarded as historical fact. "No single example can be produced of belief in the resurrection of a historical personage such as Jesus was; none at least on which anything was ever founded. . . .

34

The Christian Resurrection is thus a fact without historical analogy." [1]

It might be argued that, even if this is so, these legends of dying and rising gods might have prepared the disciples' minds for an expectation of their Master's rising from the dead, and so made it easy for them to imagine that they had seen Him. But this argument must also fail. In addition to the two points noted in the two preceding paragraphs, we shall later have to take note of what is said in chapters 5 and 6 concerning the fact of the empty tomb and the reality of the appearances of the risen Jesus.

We conclude with the affirmation that, even when the testimony of the documents is brought down to its irreducible minimum, it still makes plain that from its beginning the Church believed that Jesus had been raised from the dead, and strongly suggests that that belief cannot be accounted for except on the assumption that He had so been raised.

[1] Orr, *The Resurrection of Jesus.*, p. 224.

CHAPTER FOUR

DIFFICULTIES IN THE GOSPEL NARRATIVES

When we read through the four Gospel accounts of the Easter happenings, we can scarcely fail to be impressed by the solid mass of agreement they present on the main points. We shall find, for instance, that all four are in accord on these points:

(1) That Jesus was crucified on the Friday of Passover week.

(2) That Joseph of Arimathea successfully petitioned Pilate for permission to bury the body of the dead Jesus.

(3) That the body was swathed in linen, as the custom was, before burial.

(4) That burial was made in a "rock" tomb. (Only John, in his account of the burial, fails to mention explicitly the nature of the tomb, but his reference in 20 : 1 to the stone being rolled away implies it.)

(5) That women followers of Jesus visited His tomb early on the following Sunday.

(6) That they found that the stone sealing the grave had been rolled away, and that the body of Jesus was gone.

(7) That a message was given them there that Jesus was risen.

(8) That the Risen Jesus appeared to His followers (to individuals and to groups)

a number of times between that day and Pentecost.

There are, further, a number of subsidiary points upon which there is no disagreement; points for example, which may be mentioned by one or two or three Gospels only but are not at variance with anything said in the remaining three or two or one—such as the mention by Matthew, Mark and Luke that the women were onlookers at the burial of Jesus, or the mention by Matthew, Luke and John that the tomb in which Jesus was laid was a new tomb.

It must be recognized, of course, that there are points of difference between the narratives. But, on the whole, their presence strengthens rather than weakens the narratives' unmistakable ring of authenticity; for one would naturally expect to find some difference in detail between reliable, independent accounts of any event, much more of one so unusual and disturbing as this.

Reports taken from each of several eyewitnesses of any exciting event—a street accident, say, or a riot or a battle—will invariably contain differences. But, if the witnesses are honest and sincere, their reports will show agreement on the main points. This is just what we find in the Gospel narratives of the Resurrection. If the narratives had been exactly the same on every point, that would have been more disquieting, as giving grounds for suspicion that there had been a deliberate intention to avoid any suggestion of disagreement.

Let us bear in mind, after all, that, if the Resurrection is true, the disciples must on Easter Day have been in a tremendously excited condition, such as would not be at all conducive to keeping careful diary notes of every detail or even a clear mental picture of all that occurred. Even had they each written down an account of the day's events within twenty-four hours, we should not expect these accounts to be in exact agreement; and, if they had proved to be exactly the same, we should want some explanation for their being free from the minor differences, which are always to be found in such independent accounts of any event.

When we remember these things, and when we remember, in addition, that each eyewitness writes from his own point of view, and that none seeks to give an exhaustive account of everything that happened at the first Easter, we should not find it too difficult to understand why differences exist, nor to recognize in them actual marks of reliability.

Two illustrations employed by Professor James Orr[1] may assist that understanding:

A history class studying the French Revolution was asked to investigate and report on the vote by which King Louis XVI was condemned to death. Nearly half the class reported that the vote was unanimous, some that there was a majority of one, and a few that the majority was 145 in a vote of 721. At first sight, these reports seem hopelessly contradictory, even though they agree on the main point that Louis was condemned. "Yet for each the authority of reputable historians could be given. In fact, all were true, and the full truth a combination of all three." The complete story was this— that three votes were taken. The first was on the issue of the king's guilt, and was unanimous. The

[1] *Op. cit.*, p. 90 and p. 107 footnote.

next was to decide the penalty, and a majority of 145 voted in favour of the sentence of death. The final vote, which had a majority of one, decided that the sentence should be carried out at once.

"A friend is at the point of death. On returning from a journey, I am met in succession by different persons, one of whom tells me of his illness, two others inform me of his death, while a fourth gives me a parting message. In writing later to an acquaintance, I state briefly that on my way home I had met four friends, who had given me the particulars of his illness and death, and conveyed to me his last dying words. Of what interest would it be to the recipient of the letter to know whether all the friends came together or separately, which came first and which brought the message?"

Such illustrations could be multiplied, not only from history but from our own day to day experience. If, for instance, my diary records for a certain date, "Worked at sermon from 9–12.30", does it cease to be a reliable account because no mention is made of the cup of tea I had at 10.30? Yet it is sometimes on little more ground than that that the attempt is made to question the trustworthiness of the narratives of the Resurrection.

We find, for example, great play being made with the differences in the names and number of the women who visited the tomb on Easter morning. Matthew (28 : 1) speaks of "Mary Magdalene and the other Mary"; Mark (16 : 1) of "Mary Magdalene, Mary the mother of James, and Salome"; Luke (24 : 10) of Mary Magdalene, Joanna, Mary the mother of James, and other women; and John (20 : 1) only of "Mary Magdalene". Admittedly, the narratives are incomplete, but does that make them contradictory or destroy their reliability? After all, was it so very important for the first readers to know, for example, whether the women went all together to the grave or separately?

The "contradictions" in the Gospel narratives of the Resurrection are sometimes much exaggerated; but we who believe these narratives to be reliable must be careful to be honest with ourselves. There are some points which present undeniable difficulty. But the difficulties are greatly eased—if not altogether removed—by bearing in mind the factors already cited; by remembering especially the process by which the Gospels came into being; and by recognizing that, at any given point, the evangelists may have been using different forms of the tradition, or interpreting a less central part of the same tradition in somewhat different ways. The important thing is not that there are differences but that, amid all the differences of lesser detail, there is such striking unanimity on the essential facts.

Four points demand individual attention.

(a) *The Reaction of the Women*. Mark apparently differs strikingly from the other Gospels in his description of the women's behaviour after their discovery of the empty tomb. The verse which ends the authentic part of Mark's Gospel[1] reads: "And they went out and fled from the tomb; for trembling and astonishment had come upon them; and *they said nothing to any one*, for they were afraid" (Mark 16 : 8). Matthew says: "So they departed

[1] Verses 9–20 of Mark 16 are not part of the book as it came from the hand of its author. What Mark himself wrote goes no further than 16 : 8, and the remainder has been added by another hand, probably as compensation for an ending somehow lost.

quickly from the tomb with fear and great joy, *and ran to tell his disciples*" (Matthew 28 : 8); while Luke reads, "and returning from the tomb they *told all this to the eleven and to all the rest*" (Luke 24 : 9).

The seriousness of this difference is more apparent than real. In the immediately preceding verse in the Markan passage (16 : 7), the young man at the tomb commands the women, "Go, tell his disciples and Peter that he is going before you to Galilee; there you will see him, as he told you". Coming immediately after this, the words "they said nothing to any one" cannot be intended to mean absolute and permanent silence. The inclusion of this command, indeed, leaves no doubt that Mark's knowledge of the history was in harmony with that of Matthew and Luke, namely, that the women carried their story to the disciples. "They said nothing to any one" probably means no more than this, that, in their awed and trembling astonishment, they spoke to no one on the homeward way, but kept their tidings for the disciples' ears.

(*b*) **The Location of the Risen Lord's Appearances.** It is often argued that the scene of the Resurrection appearances presents us with a major discrepancy. On the one hand, so the argument runs, we have Mark (by implication) and Matthew speaking of appearances in Galilee without mention of any in Jerusalem; while, on the other, Luke and John describe appearances in or around Jerusalem without mention of any in Galilee, except for that described in John's Appendix.[1] On this point, it is alleged, our

[1] John 21 appears to have been added after the completion of the Gospel, which reaches its natural conclusion in 20 : 30–31. But this final chapter must have been added early, as there is no trace of the existence of the Gospel without it, and in general character it does not differ markedly from the rest of the Gospel.

41

records are divided into two irreconcilable camps.

It must be allowed that there is difficulty here. It should, however be pointed out that the Gospel records are not quite so rigidly divided between separate "Jerusalem" and "Galilee" traditions as might be thought. It is true that what we possess of Mark makes it almost certain that he intended to go on and speak of an appearance or appearances in Galilee; but he may well have had it in mind to speak of Jerusalem appearances as well. It is true that Matthew gives prominence in his narrative to Galilee, but he does record also an appearance to the women in Jerusalem. It is true that Luke makes no mention at all of a Galilaean appearance, but he is evidently covering the events of several days in very short compass, and his omission of any Galilaean appearance cannot be taken as certain evidence that he knew of none. It is true that the fourth Gospel mentions a Galilaean appearance only in the Appendix, but is it without significance that it is there mentioned?

A further point may be added. The fact that two Gospels concentrate on appearances in Jerusalem and two on appearances in Galilee is not equivalent to their being contradictory. Far too much is made at times of the argument from silence. The failure of one of the Gospel writers to mention any given point ought never to be taken as evidence that either he was unaware of it or did not accept it. The evangelists give no more than limited selections from the material they could have used, and their inclusion of this and omission of that was governed by the sense each had of what was most profitable to include, and by the plan underlying the writing of his book. It may still seem surprising that the writers do not all speak of appearances in both places. But this is not the capital difficulty it is sometimes represented as being. We do not have to choose between Galilee and Jerusalem as the scene of the appearances. The simplest explanation is probably the correct one—namely, that there were post-Resurrection appearances in both places, and that, for reasons of their own and on account of the narrow limits of their space, each writer gives prominence only to one or to the other.

(c) **The Messengers at the Tomb.** A point of real difference is in the descriptions of the messengers found at the empty tomb. Mark 16 : 5: "And entering the tomb, they (the women) saw a young man sitting on the right side, dressed in a white robe"; Matthew 28 : 2–3: " . . . an angel of the Lord descended from heaven and came and rolled back the stone, and sat upon it. His appearance was like lightning, and his raiment white as snow"; Luke 24 : 4: "While they (the women) were perplexed about this, behold, two men stood by them in dazzling apparel"; John 20 : 11–12: "she (Mary) stooped to look into the tomb; and she saw two angels in white, sitting where the body of Jesus had lain, one at the head and one at the feet".

It must be frankly admitted that there *is* contradiction here, and we do not know enough to be able to say with assurance how it is to be reconciled. We may say, however, that its origin and its explanation are probably to be traced back to the excitement of the unexpected happenings of that Easter morning, and to the inability of the women later to be perfectly clear on points of detail. And this is, after all, no more than a point of detail, albeit a prominent and somewhat remarkable one. The angels are secondary figures in the narrative of that morning; and concerning the main events—that the tomb was empty and that the women received tidings that Jesus was risen—there is unanimity. Our conclusion is that, although the differences between the narratives at this point may continue to puzzle us, they need not affect our faith in their fundamental trustworthiness.

(d) *Discrepancies between the Gospels and 1 Cor. 15 : 3 ff.* These apparent discrepancies may at first sight seem very serious. In the Corinthians passage, for instance, the first appearance mentioned is to Peter; there is no specific mention of the empty tomb; and there is no mention of the women. But, once again, much more importance is sometimes attached to these differences than the facts warrant.

Two points should be particularly borne in mind. One is that Paul does not seek to tabulate all the events of Easter Day, nor all the appearances of the Risen Jesus, just as the Gospels, for their part, do not each give a complete account. The other is that Paul is not seeking to prove the Resurrection to his readers, but is giving them no more than a brief reminder of facts which, for them as well as for him, are beyond doubt.

There is, therefore, no reason for taking 1 Cor. 15 : 3 ff. as a citation by Paul of all that he knows of the Church's evidence for the Resurrection, or as a full statement of all that he could have said or would have said, if the fact of the Resurrection of Jesus were being called in question and he had need to plead its truth. This being so, it is unnecessary to

44

reckon it a matter of grave concern that there should be some differences—even if, in our own lack of total knowledge, we find them difficult to harmonize—between the incomplete list of 1 Cor. 15 and the incomplete accounts in the Gospels.

We do not wish to suggest that there are no real difficulties in the Gospel narratives of the Resurrection. But the existence of difficulties is no reason for dismissing the Resurrection story, if it be seen to be in other respects credible. The real difficulty is not the "contradictions" in the Gospels. What are they, after all, compared with the tremendous agreement? The real difficulty is the supernatural character of the event concerned.

CHAPTER FIVE

THE EMPTY TOMB

On the day of the Crucifixion all was heartbreak and wretchedness among the little band of the Nazarene's followers. But over that week-end something happened that transformed them.

The first inkling of strange events was given to a handful of women. They had been faithful followers of Jesus, and had even stood at the foot of the Cross to be with their Master to the end. At length they saw Him die, and they looked on while Joseph of Arimathea placed His body in the tomb. Then they went home, with the intention of returning—not on the morrow which was the Sabbath and must, by the Jewish law, be spent resting—but on the following day, our Sunday, the first day of the week. Their purpose was to perform fully those last rites of cleansing and embalming to which Joseph and his helpers had been able to attend only hastily and partially because of the nearness of the Sabbath, which began at sunset on Friday (Luke 23 : 49–24 : 1).

Very early on Sunday morning the women made their way back to the tomb, perhaps together, perhaps separately, and found it empty.

That Jesus' grave was really empty on the Sunday morning is beyond any reasonable question. One thing alone is sufficient to make that plain. This is that, right from the beginning, the emptiness of the grave was taken for granted by friend and foe alike. What the Jews did was not to deny that the tomb was vacant, but to offer a natural explanation of the fact. "The disciples of Jesus," they alleged, "have stolen his body out of the tomb." Could the fact that the tomb was empty have any more certain confirmation than that? (Matthew 28 : 12–15).

Moreover, a mere seven weeks after the Crucifixion, the disciples of Jesus were going about the streets of Jerusalem announcing, "Our Jesus is risen from the dead." Try to imagine the scene. In the very city where their Master had been slain, and only a short distance from where His dead body had been laid to rest, the Christians were proclaiming the astounding message that He had risen. How could such tidings have gained any credence, how for that matter could they have continued to be proclaimed, if, close at hand and open to anyone's inspection, lay the tomb of Jesus and His body in it? If the tomb had still been occupied, it would have been the simplest thing in the world for the Jewish authorities to expose that fact, and so to silence the Christian message.

It has been suggested that the belief that the tomb was empty may have originated through a mistake on the part of the women. The following is the reconstruction that is made of events: Coming as they did, in the uncertain light of very early morning and with many tombs more or less similar round about, the women went to the wrong one. By chance the one they chose was lying open and empty, and had a young man standing in or beside it, the gardener perhaps. He, guessing the women's errand and realizing the mistake they had made, attempted to direct them to the right tomb. Pointing it out, he said, "He whom you seek is not here. There is the place where they laid Him." But the women were by now so frightened, with such a succession of unexpected events added to the strangeness of the circumstances, that they only imperfectly understood before they turned in flight. Later, the conjecture continues, when belief in the Lord's Resurrection arose on other grounds (viz. the disciples' belief that He had appeared to them), the women, looking back on their experience, interpreted it as the Gospels now record it.

This theory, advocated by Kirsopp Lake, is ingenious, but it does not really meet the facts. The Gospel narratives give unanimous and emphatic testimony that it was Jesus' tomb the women visited, and offer no shred of support for Lake's theory, which is pure conjecture. Would it not demand a most remarkable combination of coincidences that (1) the women should happen to make a mistake in the tomb; (2) the tomb visited in error should happen to be lying open and empty; (3) there should happen to be someone at this very tomb at that precise hour, even though it was so very early an hour; and (4) this stranger should happen instantly to divine their mistake and try to put them right? Moreover, is it not extremely improbable that no one else should ever go to see the tomb? Surely, for instance, some of the disciples would wish to verify the report of the vacant grave—which, in fact, the narratives tell us that they did. And, even if we were to assume that neither did any of the women nor any of the disciples ever return to the tomb, we could not imagine that those who were hostile to the new movement would be so careless. They would not be prepared simply to take the Christians' word for it that the tomb was empty. We may be sure that, had the women erred and the body of Jesus still lain in the grave, the error would quickly have been exposed.

It is sometimes alleged that Paul knew nothing of the empty tomb—a deduction drawn from the fact that he makes no explicit mention of it in 1 Cor. 15. But there was no reason why Paul should mention it. He was seeking neither to prove the truth of the Resurrection nor to give a detailed list of all the factors in the story, as if he were telling it for the first time. He was simply recalling to the Corinthians what he had previously told them, and what he could take for granted as part of their belief. In any case, the sequence of his words implies an empty tomb: "Christ died . . . was buried . . . rose again." What point is there otherwise in the middle reference "was buried"?

Other explanations have, of course, been attempted. The earliest was that put forward by the Jews to the effect that the disciples had stolen the body, and from time to time this accusation has been taken up once more. But we have already considered the difficulties involved in this view. No theory of the removal of the body by friends of Jesus can reasonably be entertained. And had it been removed by others who were not His followers, the fact must speedily have been published. If, for instance, the Jewish authorities had moved the body or prevailed on Pilate to do so (perhaps to avoid possible veneration of the tomb), as soon as the Resurrection preaching began this would have been announced, and scornful fingers pointed to the actual resting-place of the remains of Him who was affirmed to have risen.

There are other arguments against the view that the body of Jesus had been removed by human hands, whether those of friend or foe. There are the practical difficulties of the removal, which must have involved a number of men and have been carried out at dead of night. There is the curious circumstance that, despite the need for secrecy and the consequent desire for speed, these men apparently took time to unwrap the grave-clothes from the corpse (John 20 : 6–7). But it will already be plain that no such theory can seriously be upheld.

Another alternative explanation is provided by "the swoon theory". This has long been discredited, so that it is now, in Frank Morison's words, "really little more than an historical curiosity".[1] But some form of the theory is still apt to present itself to minds that struggle with doubts.

First put forward by the rationalist Venturini at the beginning of the 19th century, the swoon theory owed its origin to the strength of the evidence for the empty tomb. Faced with the necessity either of accepting the Christian explanation or of finding an alternative explanation, some have suggested that perhaps Jesus did not really die on the Cross, but only fainted; and that, reviving in the cool of the tomb, making His escape and returning to His disciples, He inspired them with a belief that He had been raised from the dead.

The basic presumption of this theory—the idea that Jesus did not really die on the Cross—is one of extreme improbability. When Jesus was taken down

[1] *Who Moved the Stone?*, p. 89.

from the Cross, those supervising His execution were convinced that the job was done; and if they, whose duty it was to know, were satisfied that He was dead, it is hardly likely that they were mistaken.

However, supposing that for the sake of argument we concede that Jesus may have been, not dead, but merely in a swoon when taken from the Cross and placed in Joseph's tomb, think what the theory requires us to believe! Arrested the previous evening, Jesus had been up all night. He had been subjected, through the night and early morning hours, to a continuous attack involving severe mental and nervous strain. He had been not only without sleep but without food and drink during that time. He had been exposed to the dreadful blood-letting and strength-sapping punishment of the flagellum (a whip of several thongs whose ends were loaded with lead). Already so weak that He was unable, as was customary, to carry His own Cross to the place of execution, He had then been crucified, stretched out on that terrible instrument of death and left there to hang in agony through the mounting heat of the day. He had been run through with a soldier's spear, before His body was taken down from the Cross. He had been wrapped round and round with yards and yards of bandages, inlaid with a hundred pounds' weight of spices; and finally had been placed in a tomb across whose entrance its massive stone door had been rolled. What we are required to believe is that this Jesus, who had come so near to death without actually dying, and who must have been in a seriously weakened condition as a result of His sufferings and His wounds, somehow regained consciousness in the tomb, somehow—weak as He was—struggled free from the mass of linen enswathing Him, and, though unaided and working from the difficult inside position, rolled back the stone which shut Him in, and made His way unseen to His disciples. Is it credible?

Let us again suppose, for the sake of argument, that this might have happened. Can we imagine that such a returned Jesus—naked, weak and well-nigh helpless—could have inspired in His disciples a belief that He was conqueror of death? It was on just this point, a century ago, that Strauss, himself a sceptic, dealt a mortal blow to the swoon theory. "It is evident," he wrote, "that this view of the Resurrection of Jesus, apart from the difficulties in which it is involved, does not even solve the problem which is here under consideration—the origin, that is, of the Christian Church by faith in the miraculous Resurrection of a Messiah. It is impossible that a being who had stolen half-dead out of the sepulchre, who crept about weak and ill, wanting medical treatment, who required bandaging, strengthening and indulgence, and who still at last yielded to His sufferings, could have given to the disciples the impression that He was a conqueror over death and the grave, the Prince of Life, an impression which lay at the bottom of their future ministry." [1]

Finally, let us recall what Henry Latham calls the "witness of the grave-clothes", because this is witness that tells not only against the swoon theory but against all attempted "natural" explanations of the empty tomb. From a careful study of John 20 : 1–10 in its original Greek, particularly with reference to the words "lying" and "rolled up", Latham is

[1] D. F. Strauss, *New Life of Jesus*, p. 412.

52

convinced that the position of the grave-clothes left in the tomb was most significant. The narrative runs, "Then Simon Peter came, following him, and he went into the tomb; he saw the linen cloths lying, and the napkin, which had been on his head, not lying with the linen cloths but rolled up in a place by itself" (John 20 : 6–7). The Greek verbs strongly suggest, asserts Latham, that the grave-clothes[1] were found undisturbed. They were not disarranged, nor thrown aside. It was not even that they had been neatly folded up and placed in separate heaps. They were lying just as they had been when placed around the body of Jesus—except that the body had gone.

"When Jesus rose from the dead, He withdrew from the grave clothes without disturbing their arrangement; on His retiring from them, the linen clothes fell flat on the rock, because their support was withdrawn, and because they were borne down by the hundred pounds' weight of aloes and myrrh (John 19 : 39). But there was no such weight pressing upon the napkin. Its smaller size or the nature of its material, or its three days' wrapping, or all these, united together, apparently enabled it to retain its erect form after the support which had moulded it was withdrawn." [2] The witness of the grave-clothes is twofold. Against all efforts to explain the empty tomb in some "natural", non-miraculous way, it asks, first, "How did the grave-clothes come to be left in the tomb?" and, second, "How is it that they lay as they did?"

The incontrovertible fact of the empty tomb is one

[1] The grave-clothes would, according to the Eastern fashion, be in two separate portions, those covering the body and those round the head, with the face, neck and shoulders left bare.
[2] *The Risen Master*, p. 3.

of the major evidences for the Resurrection. On the rock of this stubborn piece of history, many of the fiercest attacks on it have been broken; for the fact that the tomb was empty can only mean that Jesus had indeed been raised from the dead. It can be satisfactorily explained in no other way. Confirmatory of this conclusion is the fact that the best the Jewish leaders could do was to put forth the false statement that the disciples had stolen the body. Now, these stern opponents of the preaching of the Resurrection numbered in their ranks some of the ablest minds of the day, men of keen intellect, of legal training, and thoroughly versed in the science of argument. In addition they possessed all the facts of the case from the hostile viewpoint. These men, indeed, being on the spot and having access to all the information, and being possessed, not only of undoubted ability but also of undoubted hatred of the Christian cause, were the men best able in all history to put forward a case, if it were possible, that would disprove the Resurrection. Yet the best explanation that they could offer of the empty tomb[1] was the suggestion that the disciples had stolen the body. That their best was so poor shows that the facts were against them. Jesus was risen indeed.

---

[1] The tomb in which Jesus was laid was very different from those graves to which most of us are accustomed. Like many of that time, some of which are still to be seen around Jerusalem, it consisted of a large cave, hewn out of the rock. A ledge on the side of the cave served as a resting-place for the body (or perhaps there would be several ledges). The entrance to the tomb was an opening about 4 ft. by 2 ft. in size, and its door was a circular stone, something like a large grindstone, which was propelled backwards and forwards along a grove running past the cave mouth.

CHAPTER SIX

THE APPEARANCES OF THE RISEN LORD

We may well regret that the Gospels give only small selections of reminiscences concerning Jesus. We ought, nevertheless, to be grateful for what they do record, and particularly glad that the New Testament makes mention of no less than ten appearances of Jesus between Easter Day and Ascension Day. These are:

(1) To Mary Magdalene: John 20 : 1–18 (Mark 16 : 9).

(2) To the Women: Matthew 28 : 1–10.

(3) To Peter: 1 Cor. 15 : 5; Luke 24 : 34.

(4) To the disciples on the road to Emmaus: Luke 24 : 13–31 (Mark 16 : 12–13).

(5–8) To the Eleven and Other Disciples:

    (a) Luke 24 : 36–49; John 20 : 19–23; 1 Cor. 15 : 5 (Mark 16 : 14–18).

    (b) John 20 : 24–29.

    (c) Matthew 28 : 16–20; 1 Cor. 15 : 6.

    (d) Luke 24 : 50–53; Acts 1 : 3–9 (Mark 16 : 19–20).

(9) To Seven Disciples: John 21 : 1–14.

(10) To James: 1 Cor. 15 : 7.

On the Sunday morning after the Crucifixion, the tomb of Jesus was found empty and His body gone. The empty tomb alone would not have produced an immediate, clear conviction that Jesus had risen.

It would have occasioned only bewilderment. But something more happened on that Sunday, which explained why the tomb had been found empty, and which was to send Jesus' friends into the streets of Jerusalem and beyond with the message of the Resurrection.

What was this "something more"? The New Testament witness is that, on the same day on which the tomb was found empty, Jesus appeared alive to some of His friends, and that, during the next six weeks, He was seen and spoken with several times. He would appear to one of the intimate band, or to a group of them; sometimes to some of the larger band of followers, once even to five hundred of them gathered together. Remembering how the Gospels give no more than selections, we may take it as reasonably probable that the ten recorded appearances constitute only a part of the appearances that actually took place. Together they constitute testimony to the Resurrection that has to be taken very seriously indeed.

In considering this testimony, we may take it for granted that the disciples really believed that Jesus had appeared to them. But while the reality of the belief is not contested, the reality of the appearances is, and many theories have been advanced to explain them. All of these are variants of one main alternative, and may be termed "Hallucination Theories". The basic contention is that, although the disciples were genuinely under the impression that they had seen the Risen Jesus, it was their imagination that had led them astray.

So impressed had they been by Jesus, runs the theory, that they were expecting Him to conquer death; this expectation took such hold of their minds that they imagined that they saw Him. It did not take much to set the process in motion. Mary Magdalene probably began it. In the garden she fancied that she saw the Risen Lord. This was all that was needed for others to catch the infection; and hallucination followed hallucination.

At first sight, this theory is not unattractive. But no form of it will pass a close examination.

It is the primary presumption of any theory of hallucinations that the disciples were expecting Jesus to rise. But this essential condition was not fulfilled. The disciples were *not* expecting the Resurrection; far from it. Good Friday left them utterly defeated, broken in heart, crushed in spirit and quite without hope. He, round whom they had woven such dreams, had been executed with ignominy, and their dreams were shattered. Jesus had failed, shamefully failed, and the best they could hope for now was to save their own skins. Their mood was the reverse of what was required to prompt visions of a Risen Jesus. They were only too dismally sure that they had seen the last of Him.

So far from being in an eagerly responsive state of mind, they were actually reluctant to accept the fact of the Resurrection even after it had occurred. Here was no body of men ready to snatch at straws and quick to embrace any suggestion of Resurrection. On the contrary, when the women came with their tale that Jesus was alive, they would not believe them—"these words seemed to them an idle tale, and they did not believe them" (Luke 24 : 11). And one of them, at least, was disposed to be sceptical even after the Risen Jesus had shown Himself. "Now Thomas

57

. . . was not with them when Jesus came. So the other disciples told him, 'We have seen the Lord.' But he said to them, 'Unless I see in his hands the print of the nails, and place my finger in the mark of the nails, and place my hand in his side, I will not believe.' " (John 20 : 24–25; and see also Matthew 28 : 17; "When they saw him they worshipped him; but some doubted.") So uncomplimentary are these references to some who were numbered among Jesus' closest friends that they could never have found their way into the accounts unless they depicted historical truth; and they make it plain that, far from being expected, the Resurrection took the disciples so much by surprise that their first reaction was an unwillingness to believe:

"But," it may be said, "did not Jesus make prophecies that He would rise, and would not these create in their minds an expectation of His Resurrection?" It seems beyond doubt that Jesus did foretell His Resurrection to His disciples. But it seems equally certain that they did not understand. Even in the Gospels, written as they were with the full light of Easter thrown back upon their events, Jesus' sayings concerning the Resurrection are neither very explicit nor very prominent. This is an indication of how little they were understood at the time that they were spoken. Whether it was that Jesus deliberately refrained from making His language too definite, or that the idea was too strange and too difficult, the disciples failed to grasp what He was trying to tell them. Perhaps the latter reason is the more likely. They refused to take Jesus seriously when He tried to warn them of His approaching death; and, if they were slow and unwilling to understand that, how could they possibly grasp His teaching concerning the Resurrection that was to follow? At any rate, Jesus' endeavours to let them know what lay ahead were largely unavailing, and when the blow fell and the Crucifixion came, it took them unawares and left them shattered.

It may be well, at this point, to retrace some ground and restate that there is no foundation for the affirmation sometimes made that history contains many instances analogous with the Resurrection of Jesus. Not uncommonly, it is said, men were supposed in ancient times to have survived death; and it is, therefore, readily understandable that the disciples, armed with the thesis that "heroes do not die",[1] should be ready and responsive subjects for hallucinations of a Risen Jesus.

But it is not the case that there are numerous legends of Resurrection. Renan declares, "Heroes do not die. . . . At the moment when Mohammed expired, Omar issued from the tent, sabre in hand, and declared he would strike off the head of any one who would dare to say that the Prophet was no more".[2] James Orr comments, "But heroes *do* die, and the parallel is without relevance. Mohammed's followers never seriously claimed that the Prophet did not die, or had risen from the dead. There is no instance in history, apart from Christianity, of a religion established on belief in the Resurrection of its Founder." [3]

We note now some features in the Gospel narratives which are very difficult to square with the idea that the Resurrection appearances of Jesus were due to hallucination.

[1] Renan, *Les Apôtres*, p. 3.   [2] *ibid.*   [3] *op. cit.*, p. 146.

The disciples as pictured in the Gospels do not at all give the impression of people likely to fall a prey to hallucinations. For hallucinations are the product of nervous minds, and are communicated by suggestion to other nervous minds. The women, it is true, might be regarded as possible victims of hallucination; but the men, in the main a practical and unimaginative lot, are not such likely subjects of hysteria and fanciful flights of imagination as the hallucination theory would make them out to be.

The circumstances of the appearances do not conform to what a theory of hallucinations would lead us to expect. There is no trace of mass suggestion, with the fantasy of one highly-strung mind being multiplied in others. What we actually have is a number of appearances that take place independently, to different individuals or groups, at different times and in different places.

Hallucinations are usually momentary things. But the appearances of Jesus are no mere fleeting glimpses. Not infrequently He stays with His friends for a considerable time.

The appearances do not become increasingly extravagant and increasingly numerous, as is the usual way with hallucinations. Rather are they remarkably restrained in character and, far from developing a feverishly mounting frequency over a considerable period, cease altogether after about six weeks. And not only do they cease soon, they cease abruptly, whereas hallucinations usually run a fever-like course, rising to a peak and then tailing gradually away.

The appearances seem to have an "ordered" character. So far as our knowledge goes, they would seem to have taken place at progressively greater distances from the grave, beginning at the grave itself, moving further afield, and coming to an end as soon as the disciples had clearly recognized that their Risen Master was limited no longer to any one place at any one time. If the appearances had been the creation of the disciples' minds, one would have expected them to be somewhat indiscriminate and haphazard in their occurrence. But this does not seem to have been the case. On the contrary, there is a marked suggestion of purpose underlying the manner in which they took the disciples further and further from the tomb, until they left them finally with the clear conviction that their Lord was liberated from the limitations of time and space. Does not this suggest that their origin lay in something outside the disciples' own thoughts and expectations and that, in fact, this feature of the appearances makes plain Jesus' deliberate intention to leave them with this very conviction of His omnipresence, a conviction which was essential to their future ministry and its success?

The result of the appearances on the thought and conduct of the disciples is contrary to what hallucinations would be expected to produce. Hallucinations could hardly have left them so clear-headed in their belief about Jesus, so purposeful in following Him and so energetic in preaching Him. A. B. Bruce summarizes thus the judgment of Theodor Keim: "The excitement which created the visions ought to have lasted a considerable time, to have cooled down gradually, and to have terminated not in illumination and energy, but in dullness, languor and apathy"[1]; and in his own words, Keim concludes, "If therefore there

[1] *Apologetics*, p. 391.

was actually an early, an immediate transition from the visions to a calm self-possession, and to a self-possessed energy, then the visions did not proceed from self-generated visionary over-excitement and fanatical agitation among the multitude."[1]

It may be of interest, before closing the chapter, to refer to one famous variant of the hallucination theory, maintained among others by Theodor Keim, who has been cited in the preceding paragraph.[2] Some writers, of whom Keim is chief, acknowledging that the appearances must have been more than subjective visions, but unwilling to admit the full Resurrection claim, have tried to steer a middle course. Keim's attempt at compromise is the suggestion that, while Jesus' body slept on in the tomb, His spirit imparted to the disciples visions that assured them that He had conquered death. He sent "telegrams from heaven", in the form of *objective* visions. What the disciples saw was not a fantasy generated in their own minds, but something that had independent reality. It was, nevertheless, visionary, and does not require us to believe in more than the survival of Jesus' spirit.

This is a curious theory. It does, admittedly, keep clear of the impossible position that the appearances were nothing more than subjective images. But, otherwise, it seems not to relieve the difficulties which occasion it, but rather to aggravate them. The mainspring of this theory is its wish to lessen the supernormal in the Resurrection. But the "telegrams from heaven" are also a supernormal phenomenon. It is difficult to understand how, from this point

[1] Quoted in Orr, *op. cit.*, p. 226.
[2] *History of Jesus of Nazara* (1867–1872).

of view, Keim and his friends find the "telegrams" easier of belief than the Resurrection itself.

In any case, this type of theory, postulating God-given visions rather than "hallucinations", is destroyed, no less completely than the other, by the nature of the facts it is required to explain. The character of the appearances and the apostolic witness concerning them refuse to be tailored to a shape that will fit Keim's cloak; and there still remains the fact of the empty tomb, which cannot be squared with any theory of hallucinations or mere visions, whether subjective or objective.

CHAPTER SEVEN

THE NATURE OF CHRIST'S RESURRECTION BODY

We believe that what has been said in these pages is adequate to show that our Lord's Resurrection is solid historical fact. But it would be idle to suggest that no problems remain in connection with the Resurrection story. One is the difficulty of understanding just what Christ's risen body was like.

In considering this difficulty, we do not profess to be able to remove it. A full explanation would seem to be beyond the reach of the human mind at present. But there are some things worth saying.

The first is that the historical truth of the Resurrection is not affected by any difficulty of understanding, or explaining, problems associated with it. Although this may seem an obvious point, it needs to be made. We find on the one hand believers troubled, and on the other unbelievers critical, because they cannot be given a completely satisfying explanation of what is sometimes called the "mode" of the Resurrection. But this does not alter the *fact* of the Resurrection—any more than my inability to explain just how the sun exerts a pull on the earth alters the fact that it does. To regard a "satisfying explanation of the mode of the Resurrection" as a necessary preliminary to belief in the Resurrection is to take a topsy-turvy view. The attempt to obtain such an explanation becomes relevant only after the fact is established.

A second point is this. In examining the nature of Christ's Resurrection body, let us get rid of the idea that it must necessarily lie within the grasp of our limited human understanding. We ought not to insist that the risen body of our Lord be moulded into something that our minds can comprehend. Even before the Resurrection, Jesus, although subject to what are commonly called "the laws of nature", was yet able to use them in ways that we cannot repeat and often cannot understand. Why, then, need we think of Him as more limited afterwards?

Thirdly, our endeavour should be to formulate a theory which will fit the facts, and not to fit the facts into some particular theory—an error into which many people have strayed. Neglecting our second point and assuming that the risen body must belong to some already defined, intelligible category, they conclude that there are only two possibilities—either it was physical; or it was phantasmal, a mere appearance without reality. They choose one or the other, and having made their choice are driven to do violence to the facts in the interests of their theory.

Neither of these theories gives the final explanation; the truth would appear to lie somewhere between them. The facts appear to disallow the possibility that the Risen Jesus was simply either "flesh" or "spirit". The true explanation, whatever it may be, must take account of three main facts: (1) the tomb was left empty; (2) during the "forty days" (Acts 1 : 3) the Risen Jesus displayed physical attributes, being, for example, visible, tangible and audible; and (3) during the same forty days, the

Risen Jesus displayed non-physical attributes, being, for example, able to appear and disappear at will.

In the end, we can, perhaps, do no better in attempting to describe our Lord's risen body than to call it a "spiritual" body, thus borrowing, somewhat arbitrarily, the phrase Paul employs in 1 Cor. 15 of the Christian's resurrection state. It is, of course, strictly speaking, no explanation simply to state that, in the Resurrection, Jesus' physical body became a spiritual body. This does not tell us how the transformation took place, nor what exactly is a "spiritual body". The mystery remains mystery still. But this seems, nevertheless, the most helpful way of contemplating it, and leads to an easing of some of the problems involved. For by "spiritual body" we do not mean something that is purely spirit as opposed to matter. Rather do we mean to say that the physical body of Jesus became, in the Resurrection, a body that was the perfect, unhindered instrument of His spirit, no longer subject to limitations which were necessarily there in the days of His flesh. One consequence is that the difficulties of reconciling the apparently contradictory features of the "forty days" period become much less acute. It does not explain how Jesus' body, during that period, displayed both material and non-material characteristics, but it does make the fact much less difficult to accept.

In Luke 24 : 36–39, for instance, we read, "As they were saying this, Jesus himself stood among them. But they were startled and frightened, and supposed that they saw a spirit. And he said to them, 'Why are you troubled, and why do questionings rise in your hearts? See my hands and my feet, that it is I myself; handle me, and see; for a spirit has not flesh and bones as you see that I have.' " In this one incident, the same Risen Lord who suddenly and mysteriously "stood among them", also showed them his hands and his feet. But what seems, at first, a serious difficulty is seen to be no cause for anxiety, if we understand that Jesus' body is now become a "spiritual body", a body no longer subject to the laws that govern us. As Westcott puts it, "The Lord rose from the grave: and those who had known Him before, knew that He was the same and yet changed".[1] That which appeared to the disciples was really Jesus and not a disembodied spirit; yet what they saw was different from the body of flesh and superior to the laws of flesh.

Another way to describe Christ's Resurrection body is to speak of it as a "glorified" body, and this description may help to make our meaning clearer. For it may conserve, better even than "spiritual body" does, the double idea of continuity and transformation. It was still Jesus, but it was not simply His physical body restored to the old life. Neither was it a disembodied spirit—the body that had lain in the tomb was taken up into this Risen Jesus—but some wonderful change had taken place so that now it was "suited to the conditions of a higher life as our flesh-and-blood body is suited to this one".[2]

Two conclusions would seem to be implicit in this. One is that the raising of the whole Jesus, body and spirit together, so that no part was left behind and that thus the grave was left empty, demonstrated as perhaps nothing else could have done the reality and completeness of His victory over death. A second is

---

[1] *Gospel of the Resurrection*, p. 158.
[2] A. M. Hunter, *The Work and Words of Jesus*, p. 128.

that the transformation of His body points forward to that ultimate complete transformation of human nature, in which spirit shall be utterly dominant over matter, towards which the purposes of God are moving in and through the Risen Christ, and to which, in the end, He shall "raise it up".   .

It is no doubt dangerous to make too many inferences from Jesus' Resurrection to our own. For our resurrection must be in many points unlike His. But some things would seem to follow without question. In the resurrection of the individual Christian, too, it would appear—and Paul is in agreement—there shall be both continuity and difference. For us, too, the resurrection will be in a real sense the resurrection of the body—not in the sense of any continuity of the mere material elements of our present body, but in the sense of our not being unclothed spirits and of our essential person being preserved. Our resurrection body will be quite different from our present body and yet there will be identity—such as, says Paul, there exists between seed and corn. And this must be added. The resurrection of the Christian can neither be thought of apart from the Risen Christ, nor can it be thought of apart from the resurrection of all other Christians. It cannot be thought of in terms of an isolated or purely individual occurrence, for in the resurrection of the dead "the goal of the individual and the goal of the redeemed society find their perfect coincidence".[1]

But, to return to the mystery of Jesus' Resurrection body, we must confess that, though all were said that might be said, it would remain mystery still.

How the Resurrection took place we do not know,

[1] A. M. Ramsey, *The Resurrection of Christ*, p. 114.

are not yet able to know. Neither do we know how it was that Jesus in His appearance to the disciples displayed characteristics, now of flesh, now of spirit. The old idea, to which Orr gives expression, was that the forty days between the Resurrection and the Ascension were a transition period, in which Jesus' body was in an intermediate state—"no longer merely natural yet not fully entered into the state of glorification. It presents characters, requisite for the proof of its identity, which show that the earthly condition is still not wholly parted with. It discovers qualities and powers which reveal that the supraterrestrial condition is already begun."[1] It is much more likely, as Westcott would have it, that the body of Jesus was already completely changed into its "spiritual" or "glorified" condition, already the completely free and perfect instrument of His Spirit, and that such features of the "forty days" as its being audible and tangible and visible were "evidential accommodations made for the disciples' sakes".[2] But we do not know.

All attempts to solve the mystery of the "mode" of the Resurrection are interesting. But they are not vital. It is, after all, not of any great or urgent consequence that we should understand exactly how our Lord was raised or exactly what was that form in which He appeared to His disciples. The important thing, and the sufficient thing, is to know that He was raised— not, as Lazarus was raised, to a mere resumption of former life, nor in the sense of a mere survival of the soul, but in a manner which meant complete victory over death, in a manner which left His tomb empty and which saw spirit and body joined in a perfect union, which was Jesus still but was mortal flesh no longer.

[1] *The Resurrection of Jesus*, p. 196.
[2] A. M. Ramsey, *The Resurrection of Christ*, p. 46.

CHAPTER EIGHT

THE TESTIMONY OF THE CHURCH'S BEGINNING

This chapter takes up some questions concerning the Church's beginning that can find answer only in the fact of the Resurrection.

(1) *What else can explain the transformation of the disciples?* A tremendous change took place in the mind and outlook of Jesus' followers over Easter week-end. The day of the Cross left them broken-hearted and in despair. He whom they had believed to be the Messiah was dead; the glorious adventure in which they had engaged with Him had come to a bitter, ignominious end; and so they skulked behind closed doors "for fear of the Jews", afraid that, if they were unwary, they would share their Leader's fate.

But a few days later they are scarcely recognizable as the same persons. Their despair and disappointment have given place to exultation, and soon they are out in the busy streets of Jerusalem, the very citadel of their enemies, fearlessly announcing that Jesus is Risen and that He is Lord.

What has made the difference? Some wonderful experience must have befallen them since Good Friday night, and what else can it be save what they said it was—the discovery that their Master was risen from the grave? The striking change in them is a psychological miracle, which needs the miracle of the Resurrection to explain it.

(2) *What else can explain the birth of the Church?* Easter Day was the birthday of the Church, and it was the Resurrection that brought it into being.

If the dead, crucified body of their Master had been the last His followers saw of Him, it seems certain that, at the earliest opportunity, they would all have slipped away home and back to their former occupations. They would, perhaps, carry in their memories some lovely pictures of their association with the young prophet of Galilee, and in their hearts some pathetic yearnings for the days that were gone. But all such thoughts would be as of things that were past for ever. Over and above everything else would be their all too vivid recollection of the shocking end. Sometimes, perhaps, when they were in one another's company, they might indulge in reminiscence of those days that had promised so much. One thing, however, is certain. They would take care not to talk about Jesus or their own association with Him to people who had not been His followers, for this would be to invite their scorn, if not their anger. As for publicly preaching Him, they would not dare. In any case, what had they to preach? Only a story whose conclusion was tragedy and defeat. And as for suggesting to others that they should cast in their lot with this Jesus, that would be mere folly; for He was dead and gone.

It seems that this is the course that events must have run. Little mention would ever have been made again of Jesus of Nazareth. But everyone knows that in actual fact the course of history was utterly different. Shortly after the sorrow and the heartbreak of Calvary, the followers of Jesus blazed into a very fire of fearless action. They have not scattered and returned to their old haunts and their old jobs; on the contrary, history finds them together and filled with joy, united in an evangelical crusade, in the very city where the Crucifixion had taken place. At every opportunity they are shouting forth the name of Jesus and calling on others to follow Him—to follow not a dead hero, but a living Saviour.

On the one hand, we have the picture of what seems bound to have happened if the Cross had been the end of Jesus; on the other, we have history's picture of what did happen. What can explain the turn of events other than the Lord's Resurrection?

(3) *What else can explain the survival and growth of the Church?* Assuming that it could have come into being at all, it is hard to imagine that the Church could have lived very long if the Resurrection were not true. In its beginning it was a tiny minority set in the midst of bitter enmity. The number of Christ's followers gathered together in Jerusalem was a mere 120 when the preaching began (Acts 1 : 15), and they were not only in hostile territory, they were in the very stronghold of the foe. Jerusalem was the home of those who most hated the name of Jesus and had, indeed, brought about His death—the Jewish officials, the high priests, the Pharisees and the rest. Their chief ambition was to stamp out the Resurrection preaching, and everything was in their favour —power, prestige, influence, authority, organization. But what favoured them most, if the Resurrection were not true, was the foolishness of bringing the Church into being in Jerusalem, the very place where it would be simplest to prove its testimony false. If the

Resurrection were untrue, could anything have been easier than for the Jewish opposition, with all their resources and all their ability, to burst the Christian bubble at the outset?

Let us try to visualize the situation in Jerusalem, when the proclamation of the Resurrection commenced. The Jewish opposition would be violently angry (for they had thought, once they had slain Jesus, that the nuisance was at an end), and desperately keen to put a stop to the preaching. They were, moreover, some of the country's keenest intellects and most brilliant debaters. Mercilessly the story would be investigated, from every angle and in an ultra-critical spirit; and any weakness would be exploited to the full. What chance of survival did it have, if it were not true, in Jerusalem of all places, where evidence of its falseness must be lying to hand, and where opposition of this deadliest kind confronted it? Here we have well-trained lawyers, men versed in the use of argument and the science of debate; and there a group of ordinary people, a few with some education, most with little or none. These were the gladiators who faced one another in the arena of Jerusalem's streets, some nineteen hundred years ago. The odds were all in favour of the lawyers. But they lost. Could they have lost, unless the cause against which they were fighting was the truth?

The Church did not merely survive. It grew. This means not only that the case for the truth of the Resurrection was too strong for its enemies to disprove, but also that it was strong enough to convince many who were sceptical or indifferent. The Church gained ground at an astonishing pace. In little more than a generation it had spread far beyond the land of its birth, reaching into Asia Minor and Greece and even to Rome itself, and counted its adherents not in scores but in scores of thousands. Could there possibly have been such astonishing growth, if the Church's central message had been based on deceit or fraud, either voluntary or involuntary? The people won to the Church were not naturally inclined to lap up with eager credulity a story of resurrection. The prejudices of all of them, both Jew and Gentile, were strongly against believing the Christian story. The Christian preachers must have been continually engaged in debate, continually subjected to interrogation and continually under the fire of critical cross-examination concerning their startling message and the evidence they had to adduce in its support. This being so, the extraordinary number of converts speaks for itself.

And this is most noteworthy of all in respect to the remarkable progress of the Church in Jerusalem itself. Only a few weeks before the public preaching began, Jesus' career had come to an inglorious end on a gallows in that city. Many of the folk in Jerusalem to whom the first preaching was addressed must have seen Jesus in His death-throes, and all of them would be acquainted with what had happened. The Crucifixion must have seemed to them final, indisputable proof that the claims of Jesus were false. They were near to the events, both in time and in place. Accordingly, much of the Resurrection story could easily become the subject of direct investigation. The authorities, who were the leaders of the Jewish people and influenced them greatly, absolutely denied the Resurrection; pre-eminent as they were in the arts of debate and argument, they would employ their skill to the full in attacking the disciples' story, and in exploiting any apparent weakness in it. In view of all this, it is clear that the story which persuaded anyone in Jerusalem that Jesus was risen must have been such as could stand up to any criticism. That thousands of converts were made in the first few weeks must seem inexplicable unless the Resurrection story was true.

(4) *What else can explain the Observance of the First Day of the Week?* The main day of worship for the Christians was the first day of the week, that is, what we call Sunday, and not the Jewish Sabbath, which is our Saturday. We do not know exactly when the first day of the week became "worship day", because the first Christians, coming as they did from the ranks of Jewry, continued for quite a time to observe the customary Sabbath worship. But it appears that very early they began to meet together on Sunday as well for their own distinctive worship. We read, for instance, in Acts 20 : 7, that "On the first day of the week, when we were gathered together to break bread, Paul talked with them". The Jewish day was reckoned from sunset until sunset; the gathering together of the disciples probably took place on what we would call Saturday evening after sunset had ended the Sabbath and brought in the first day of the week. At first, this would be their only free period on Sunday, which was a working day; but gradually the worship of the first day of the week completely ousted, so far as the Christians were concerned, the worship of the Sabbath.

This was a remarkable happening. The earliest Christians were Jews, and converted Jews continued to form a large proportion of the Christian Church throughout the first century. Only some very outstanding consideration could have caused them to change the day of worship; what could that be other than the conviction that it was on the first day of the week that their Lord had been raised from the dead?

Additional significance may be found in the fact that it is the Book of Revelation (1 : 10) that calls the first day of the week the "Lord's day". This book was written in Asia Minor, where emperor-worship was strong and where there was a monthly festival in his honour called "Emperor's day". It is thought that this festival was a monthly commemoration of the day of the emperor's accession to the throne. This would suggest that the application of the title "Lord's day" to the first day of the week—by this time universally recognized by Christians as the day of worship—was a very pointed, even defiant, reminder that this was the day of *Christ's* accession— the day of the week that He had been raised from the dead. Says Dr. Denney, "Every Sunday as it comes round is a new argument for the Resurrection. The decisive event in the inauguration of the new religion took place on that day—an event so decisive and sure that it displaced even the Sabbath."[1]

(5) *What else can explain the conversion of the priests?* Deeply impressive as it is that in the early days the Resurrection won credence in the minds of so many of the rank and file of the Jerusalem Jews, it is even more impressive that it captured the allegiance of some of the priests (Acts 6 : 7). They were members of the party most hostile to the Christians. And they were "in the know". That is to say, they had all the information as it was represented from the enemy side, and were acquainted with all the best anti-Resurrection arguments and theories.

[1] *Jesus and the Gospel*, p. 113.

Predisposed in every way to reject the Christian claim, they were, perhaps, the least likely people to be converted to belief that history has ever known. Yet many of them were converted. Is it credible that any of them would have been so converted, unless the Christian case was so overwhelming that only an obstinate refusal to face the facts could resist it?

(6) *What else can explain the conversion of Saul?* There came a day, perhaps four years after the Crucifixion of Jesus, when a young Jew, hating the Christian faith with every fibre of his being, and harrying its adherents with every atom of his strength, turned completely round and ultimately became its most zealous and most brilliant advocate. A Rabbi and a Pharisee of excellent academic attainments, persecutor in chief, Saul was the last person anyone would have expected to become a Christian. But he did, making a change of front so remarkable that it astonished everyone (Acts 9 : 21).

The event becomes even more significant in view of the fact that Saul's hatred and untiring persecution of the Christians were allied to possession of the fullest information available to the priests. A Pharisee himself, and occupying so prominent a role in the campaign against the Resurrection preaching, he would be acquainted with all the facts as known to the Jewish headquarters, and would be well briefed in all the "natural" explanations and in all the means employed to refute the affirmation that Jesus was risen from the dead. Intellectually as well as emotionally, he was strongly predisposed against the Christian claim. Then, suddenly, he turned completely round. Having set out to exterminate the Christians in Damascus, he arrived in Damascus convinced that Jesus was risen.

What actually happened on the road to Damascus, beyond the fact that Saul had a vision of the Risen Christ, is a matter of some difference of opinion. This "appearance" was clearly different in some respects from the earlier Resurrection appearances; but Saul, at least, had no doubt that it had "independent reality"; and so, despite its differences from the others, he adds it to the list of Resurrection appearances in 1 Cor. 15. On this understanding of Saul's experience, its significance as evidence for the Resurrection is the same as that of the earlier appearances to the disciples before the Ascension. If, on the other hand, the vision existed only in Saul's mind, its evidential significance is not really a great deal less. For the crucial point is this, that it could not have come about unless Saul had grown convinced, consciously or sub-consciously, that the Resurrection story was true. And Saul of all people could never have reached this point, unless the evidence had been such as he had come to see, in spite of himself, could not reasonably be denied.

The significance of Saul's conversion may be better assessed by emphasizing four points:

(a) Saul was a man of outstanding intelligence, by common consent one of history's intellectual giants, and was also a man of extensive education and academic attainment. Here was no unthinking, unquestioning, credulous mind that might be easily captured. Here was a mind able to sift evidence, to assess experiences, and to subject alleged facts to searching scrutiny. Such a man is not likely to have been won to a faith that rested upon a deception or a few hallucinations.

(b) An exceptionally ardent Pharisee, Saul's whole training and background were such as to set him in opposition to the possibility of the Christians' being right. The mere suggestion that a crucified man could be Messiah was anathema to him, and it is not to be wondered at that he rounded in violent hatred upon those whom he was bound to regard as blasphemers and deceivers. Such a man would accept the Christian case only if he were left with no alternative.

(c) His conversion was no half-hearted affair. He did not merely begin to think that perhaps he was wrong; he became utterly convinced that they were right. He did not merely stop persecuting, he began preaching. Just as thoroughly as he had been against Christ, so now was he for Him. His conversion was such a thorough-going affair as betokened a man who was sure beyond any possibility of doubt.

(d) His conversion was not only thorough-going, it was enduring. When Saul changed his ground on the Damascus road, he changed it for life. The new course charted then was followed throughout the rest of his days, even though it cost him dear. It led him into much pain and trouble—into ridicule, hatred, persecution, stonings, floggings, imprisonments, shipwreck, death. But nothing could turn him from it and, as Frank Morison says, "You cannot explain a lifetime's practical devotion like this by 'atmospherics' or providential thunderstorms or any ephemeral or hysterical experience".[1]

(7) *What else can explain the belief in Jesus' deity?* From the start of the Church, the followers of Jesus not only called Him Saviour, they also called Him Lord; and this was to give Him equal status with God and to reckon Him divine. The Greek word for Lord, *kyrios*, originally meant someone who occupied

[1] *Who Moved the Stone?*, p. 136.

a position of authority, and was used for an "owner", for a "governor", or for "the head of a family". Later it came to be a title of address corresponding to our "sir"; and, most important for us, it came to be the word used in the Septuagint (the Greek translation of the Old Testament scriptures) to translate the Hebrew "Yahweh" or "Jehovah", thus becoming for the Jews a Greek equivalent for "God". The application of this title to Jesus carried with it the implication that He was divine.[1]

To appreciate just how extraordinary it was that Jesus should be worshipped as divine, we must remember that the first Christians were Jews. The Jews were strict monotheists and had been so for centuries. Yet here were Jews unable to resist the conviction that Jesus was divine. What a daring assertion they were making; how startlingly unorthodox it was for them to be attributing to a man born of woman a position of equality with the God of their fathers. Could anything other than the Resurrection have impelled them to it?

It may be said that the words and works of Jesus implied His deity, and that this sufficiently explains the worship accorded Him. But it is only too obvious that, prior to Easter, the disciples were in the main slow to understand Jesus and His teaching. They had come at length, it is true, to recognize Him as Messiah, but it does not seem that they had come to think of Him as divine. This required a further and a

[1] It is worth observing, also, that two common usages of *kyrios* at the beginning of the Christian era were (1) as a general description of heathen gods and (2) as a designation of the Roman Emperor. This meant that, when the title was applied to Jesus, the daring significance of that application would be readily grasped by the peoples of the Greek and Roman worlds as well as by the Jews.

greater step of faith, as orthodox Jewish thought did not generally regard the Messiah as a being of divine origin. The Messiah was to be a man specially chosen and specially endowed as the agent of God—but a man. It may be that a few, more discerning than the rest, had recognized in Jesus implications of deity. But even these would be stopped short by the disaster of the Cross.

For what makes the subsequent worship of Jesus most surprising is the fact that His life had come to such a close. No thought of deity could have survived in anybody's mind after that. That He should die at all would be serious enough; that He should die by crucifixion (to the Jews the most abhorrent of all deaths[1]) would make it doubly certain to them that any notions of Messiahship, let alone of deity, must have been terribly mistaken. Had He really been the Son of God, would not God have rescued Him from death and vindicated Him before all eyes? From the Jewish point of view, to ascribe deity to a man who had been crucified was offensive to the point of being blasphemous.

What, then, are we to make of the fact that this was actually done? Can the explanation be anything other than that God had vindicated Jesus after all? Throughout the whole book of Acts, it is made plain that to the first Christians the Cross was an object of shame and horror, which only the Resurrection had transformed. They worship Jesus not because of the Cross, but in spite of it. It was only the interpretation of the Cross in the light of the Resurrection which produced, after a time, that changed attitude to it which is to be seen, for example, in the Epistle

[1] See Deut. 21 : 22–23; Gal. 3 : 13.

to the Philippians and the Fourth Gospel, where the Cross itself is seen as the manifestation of the glory of God. Such a change could have been brought about only by an unshakable certainty in the truth of the Resurrection.

There is this further point. It was not merely that those who had followed Jesus before His Crucifixion were somehow moved to hail him as Lord after it. The history is even more remarkable yet. The Christians took their astonishing new doctrine of the deity of Jesus, and prevailed on large numbers of their countrymen to accept it. To every convert Jesus became Lord; "Jesus is Lord" was in fact, the earliest creed of the Church and in all likelihood part of the confession of faith that new members made at their baptism. What a mighty revolution it involved for these converted Jews thus to be speaking and thinking of Jesus! The suggestion, even while He lived, that Jesus was divine, would have filled nearly every Jew with repugnance; but the making of such a suggestion after the Crucifixion must have filled them with a horror so great that most of them would refuse to listen any further to what the Christians had to say. It is, therefore, of arresting import that so many who did condescend to listen, were, in spite of their angry prejudice, convinced and converted. They, too, must have been made very sure that Jesus had risen from the dead.

CHAPTER NINE

THE EVIDENCE OF BEFORE AND AFTER

Unlike the evidence already cited, what is now to be submitted might be quite reasonably explained apart from the Resurrection. It has value mainly for the Christian, who will recognize in it further confirmation of a belief already held.

(1) *The Evidence of Before: The Testimony of the Pre-Resurrection Jesus.*

It is worth remembering that "the resurrection is the resurrection of Jesus".[1] As Machen puts it, "What we are trying to establish is not the resurrection of any ordinary man . . . but the resurrection of *Jesus*. There is a tremendous presumption against the resurrection of any ordinary man, but . . . in His case the presumption is exactly reversed. It is unlikely that any ordinary man should rise, but it is unlikely that this Man should not rise."[2]

The sceptic objects that it is preposterous to suggest concerning any man that he could rise again. The Christian would agree. He does not postulate resurrection of "any man", but of Jesus Christ. Resurrection is a strange phenomenon to intrude upon human history. But, when the Person of whom it is reported is such as He, it becomes a phenomenon

[1] Denney, *Jesus and the Gospel*, p. 158.
[2] *The Christian Faith in the Modern World*, p. 227.

much less surprising. For Him it seems fitting, and not only fitting but inevitable.

That was how it appeared to the first disciples. Peter, for instance, in the course of the first Christian sermon, proclaimed of Jesus, "But God raised him up, having loosed the pangs of death, because it was not possible for him to be held by it" (Acts 2 : 24).

But have we not already declared that the Resurrection took the disciples by surprise? Indeed it did. Any idea of their Lord's rising from the dead was foreign to their thoughts before it happened. But, once they knew of it, its essential "rightness" became apparent; and, when they looked back, it seemed to them impossible that there could have been any other ending to the story.

And we, at our distance and with our perspective, are able to see even more clearly that there was never a man like this Man, and that His Person and His Resurrection are most persuasively in accord. His uniqueness is undeniable. His, for instance, was an unique character, for He alone in all history has been free from sin. "Sinlessness", is, indeed, scarcely adequate to describe His character; for sinlessness is a negative term, and Jesus' life was not only empty of evil, but also full of good. His teaching, too, was unique. "No man ever spoke like this man" was the report brought back by the agents of the chief priests and Pharisees (John 7 : 46), and their verdict has been approved by every age. His deeds, also, betokened His uniqueness. Many and wonderful were His works of healing, sometimes of body, sometimes of mind, sometimes of spirit, sometimes of all three together.

Jesus' Person itself would seem to challenge us to

accept His Resurrection as inevitable. If such as He had remained death's captive, would that not have been a denial that there was any moral basis to the universe? Would it not have made mockery of the belief that God had any part in the universe at all?

Our argument here is perhaps best summarized in a longer quotation from Denney: "If the witnesses had asserted about Herod or about any ordinary person, what they did about Jesus, the presumption would have been all against them. The moral incongruity would have discredited their testimony from the first. . . . Is it too much to infer that sometimes, when the resurrection of Jesus is rejected, the rejecter forgets that it is *this* resurrection which is in question? He thinks of resurrection in general, the resurrection of anyone; possibly he thinks of it really as the reanimation of a corpse. . . . But if he realized what Jesus means—if he had present to his mind and conscience, in His incomparable moral value, the Person whose resurrection is declared—the problem would be quite different. He might find himself far more ready, under the impression of the worth of such a person, to question the finality of his scheme of the universe; more willing to admit that, if there was not to be a perpetual contradiction at the heart of things, a perpetual extinction of the higher by the lower, such a personality must find it possible somehow to transcend the limitations of nature and its laws."[1]

(2) *The Evidence of After: The Testimony of Christian Experience.*

From the beginning of the Church, Christian men

[1] *Jesus and the Gospel*, pp. 122–3.

and women—those who, believing Jesus to be risen, have committed themselves in faith to Him—have felt conscious of their Risen Lord's presence with them, and have found themselves able to enter into a fellowship with Him that was even richer than had been possible in the days of His flesh. This has been much more than a consciousness of being inspired by His memory, as one might be inspired by the memory of a dead friend, or of being stimulated by His example, as one might be stimulated by the example of a dead hero. It has been the conviction that they had entered into an intimate relationship with One who was really alive, and who was personally active in time and space. Accompanying this conviction and testifying to its validity has been the accession of new moral power to their lives.

We have already spoken of the tremendous change in outlook and in spirit that took place in the disciples over Easter week-end, and have drawn attention to its significance. But they were altered not only emotionally and mentally but morally, too, and began to show forth qualities of a kind and to a degree that no one would have thought possible. The difference between them as they are found in the Gospels and as they are found in Acts is staggering. Ordinary men have become supermen. How? It was, at any rate, not simply the consequence of a gritting of their teeth and a girding up of their loins. They were living lives that were obviously beyond their unaided capacity. They were like men possessed. Is the truth not this, that they *were* "possessed"—by the living Christ? The change in their lives at any rate tallied with their belief that they were living in even closer fellowship with Him than before.

The same phenomenon was much in evidence throughout the primitive Church. Whenever a man came to faith in the Risen Christ, his life began to show unmistakable signs of a new element added to his moral strength. Could this have come from any source other than the Risen Christ with whom he believed that he, too, was living in fellowship?

Nor has this phenomenon of Christian experience been merely temporary. Ever since, there have been in every age—sometimes more, sometimes less—men and women who have been convinced that the Risen Christ was with them, and whose lives have given testimony to the energizing influence of fellowship with Him.

Our own day, too, has its lives that speak of new moral strength through the Risen Christ. Perhaps, indeed, there never were more such witnesses than now. All over the world, in more places and in greater numbers than ever before, there are men and women sure that the Risen Jesus is with them and prepared "to testify that when they called on the name of Jesus Christ to redeem them a new moral factor entered their lives and they became changed".[1]

From the beginning, then, Christians have felt aware of Jesus' presence, invisible but real; and their lives have seemed to suggest the possession of moral energy and power that demand explanation in something beyond themselves. Admittedly the objector may say, "This 'awareness' of Jesus' presence could be no more than a subjective feeling induced by belief in His Resurrection"—and we cannot disprove the contention. He may say again, "All these instances of moral transformation could be explained

[1] G. R. Beasley-Murray, *Christ is Alive*, p. 83.

as the psychological consequence of the conviction that Jesus is alive and that His Spirit is at work"— and we cannot prove that it is otherwise. The testimony of Christian experience, like that of the pre-Resurrection Jesus, is evidence different in kind from that of the empty tomb and the other evidences set forth earlier in this book. But neither may, on that account, be altogether set aside. They could, perhaps, be disregarded if they stood alone. But they stand alongside a mass of more objective evidence which unmistakably points to the fact of the Resurrection; and so, while they are not primary testimony and are likely to make little impression on the unbeliever, the Christian is right to find in them confirmation of his belief.

CHAPTER TEN

THE LORD IS RISEN INDEED

The contention of this book is that, in face of the evidence, it cannot reasonably be doubted that Jesus rose from the dead. We have attempted to show how evidence piling upon evidence makes that fact sure. We sum up by emphasizing the impossibility of otherwise explaining the Resurrection belief.

The real onus of making good his case, in this matter of the Resurrection, rests not with the Christian apologist but with the sceptic. The man who believes the Resurrection true is, after all, the man who accepts what the written records affirm. It is the unbeliever who is at variance with things as they are; and, if he is to justify his rejection of the belief, he is obliged to explain how it was that this belief came into existence. The belief is there and its existence—an existence which dates from the beginning—is a presumption in favour of its truth. That presumption is itself enough to carry the day, unless a satisfactory "natural" explanation is forthcoming. As Westcott has it, "Unless . . . it can be shown that the origin of the Apostolic belief in the Resurrection . . . can be satisfactorily explained on other grounds, the belief itself is a sufficient proof of the fact".[1] But there is no other satisfactory explanation.

[1] *Gospel of the Resurrection*, p. 107.

It will bring this point home to us with full force, if we start from the assumption that Jesus did not rise, and then try to work out an explanation of the existence of the belief, of the existence of the Resurrection stories, of the existence of the Church, and so on. The impossibility of the task will soon be apparent, and its implications also. For it is the simplest of propositions that, if an alleged fact is not false, it must be true.

There have been, of course, many attempts to give "other" explanations. But none of the counter-theories comes near being satisfactory, and it is interesting to observe how remarkably efficient a job they frequently make of slitting one another's throats.

In the brief compass of these pages, not all the arguments that might be adduced in favour of the Resurrection have been put forward. We hope, nevertheless, that the reader may have been helped to feel something of the strength of the evidence. For it is tremendously strong. "Indeed, taking all the evidence together," says Westcott, "it is not too much to say that there is no single historic incident better or more variously supported than the Resurrection of Christ. Nothing but the antecedent assumption that it must be false could have suggested the idea of deficiency in the proof of it."[1]

There is a story to the effect that news of the battle of Waterloo was brought by sailing ship to the south coast of England. From there the tidings were passed by semaphore to London, and in course of time the semaphore on Winchester Cathedral began to repeat it. Letter by letter it spelled out W-E-L-L-I-N-G-T-O-N D-E-F-E-A-T-E-D. Just then a blanket of fog came down

[1] *op. cit.*, p. 134.

and wrapped the signal away from sight; and far and wide across the land the news was spread that the battle had been lost. Later in the day the fog began to lift, and the despondent people saw to their surprise that the semaphore arm was moving again. This time it spelled out the completed message W-E-L-L-I-N-G-T-O-N D-E-F-E-A-T-E-D T-H-E E-N-E-M-Y. For very joy they could scarcely believe what they saw. But it was true, and soon the country rang with the gladness of apparent defeat become actual victory.

It was in somewhat similar fashion that the Easter story broke upon the world. On Good Friday the stark outline of a Cross upon a hill and the cold finality of a sealed tomb proclaimed to the beholders JESUS-DEFEATED. All week-end this was the message that hammered with cruel persistence upon the minds and spirits of His followers. But on Easter morning open grave and Risen Lord proclaimed the completed message JESUS-DEFEATED-THE-ENEMY; and gloom gave place to gladness.

It is not that the Resurrection is an overcoming of the Cross. "The Crucifixion is not a defeat needing the Resurrection to reverse it, but a victory which the Resurrection quickly follows and seals."[1] The Cross and the Resurrection are each parts of the same victorious story. But it is the Resurrection that establishes the victory and shows it forth.

And the Resurrection victory was not simply a victory limited to that particular time and place. Christ is victor to all eternity.

This means, for one thing, that His is a cause which cannot be finally defeated. Often the powers of evil

[1] A. M. Ramsey, *op. cit.*, p. 19.

91

appear to be showing themselves stronger than the powers of good, and we may be tempted to shrug our shoulders and say, "What is the use of following the good?" The Resurrection makes it plain that, however things may seem at any particular time, good is, in fact, stronger than evil and love stronger than hate, and that, in the end, these must win. If we are on the side of Christ, we are on the winning side, for the Resurrection has made it certain that somehow, sometime, God will consummate His Kingdom. We may take heart from this when we view the world, and sing, with Arthur Hugh Clough (1819–1861), this song:

> Say not—the struggle nought availeth,
> The labour and the wounds are vain,
> The enemy faints not, nor faileth—
> And as things have been, they remain!
>
> .   .   .   .   .
>
> For while the tired waves, vainly breaking,
> Seem here no painful inch to gain,
> Far back, through creeks and inlets making,
> Comes silent—flooding in—the main.
>
> And not by eastern windows only,
> When daylight comes, comes in the light;
> In front, the sun climbs slow—how slowly!
> But westward—look! the land is bright.

The Resurrection of Christ has meaning for the Christian not only in this broader sense but also in the living of his own personal life. It means that, if we have faith in the Risen Christ, we may, through living in fellowship with Him, enjoy victory in our own lives.

This means, for example, victory over sin and temptation. Our Lord's Resurrection offers us not only the opportunity to have our sins forgiven, but the opportunity also to be made stronger than they through our communion with Him. Given the chance, the Risen Christ can make new men and women of us, even of the most unlikely of us, as He did with the disciples and has done with so many since. It means, too, victory over trouble and disaster. An awareness of the companionship of the Risen Christ is able to keep a man from being defeated by the disappointments and frustrations and difficulties of every day, and to raise him triumphant above every disaster, great or small, that befalls him. It means, also, victory over fear. The knowledge of the living presence of Christ produces a serenity of mind and spirit which is more powerful than fear.

Leslie Weatherhead tells of visiting a friend who, suffering from cancer, was condemned to die. "She was a quiet and reticent soul, and it had been rather a trouble to her that, though Christ meant so much to her, she had rarely spoken of her faith to another. And then, in that room, knowing the probability of a painful death, and looking cancer right in the face, she said this, 'I am proud to be trusted with this illness. It is giving me opportunities that I never had before.' I remember saying to her, 'Well, my dear, you may not get better from cancer, but you have conquered cancer.' "[1]

The man of faith will be buffeted by life's storms

[1] *It Happened in Palestine*, p. 284.

no less than his neighbour. But by virtue of his relationship with the Risen Christ there is nothing—either in life or in death—that need finally defeat him.

W. Y. Fullerton[1] tells of climbing the mimic Calvary of the village of Domodossola in northern Italy. In ascending order up the hillside a series of chapels had been built, each depicting, with life-size terracotta figures, one of the scenes of Jesus' Passion —Jesus before Pilate, Jesus shouldering the Cross, and so on. The climax was reached with the chapel that showed Jesus hanging on the Cross, and up to this point the path running between the shrines was well-worn by the feet of countless pilgrims, come to look upon their Lord's sufferings and death. But now the path became grass-grown and was clearly little used. Dr. Fullerton, however, followed on, and, reaching the summit of the hill, found there another shrine, the Chapel of the Resurrection, which few, it was clear, took the trouble to visit. Those who built that mimic Calvary had not forgotten that Jesus rose from the tomb, but most of the pilgrims came to pay homage to a Christ who, so far as they were concerned, was dead.

And for many Christians Easter is not the day it ought to be in the calendar of their faith. They do not doubt nor disbelieve their Lord's Resurrection. But their belief has not become real to them, and they do not fully realize that Jesus *is* risen, that He *is* alive and that He *is* their constant, though invisible, companion.

The biography of the famous Congregationalist Minister R. W. Dale of Birmingham tells of his

[1] *Souls of Men*, p. 34.

working one year on his sermon for Easter Day. As he pondered his chosen theme of the Living Christ, quite suddenly its meaning broke through into his mind in a way that it had never done before. In the excitement of the revelation he leaped to his feet and began to pace his study floor, stopping now and then to appraise afresh the new insight that had come to him. Here are his own comments on the incident: " 'Christ is alive,' I said to myself. 'Alive!' and then I paused—'Alive!' and then I paused again: 'Alive! Can that really be true? Living as really as I myself am?' I got up and walked about, repeating: 'Christ is living! Christ is living!' At first it seemed strange and hardly true, but at last it came upon me as a burst of sudden glory: yes, Christ is living. *It was to me a new discovery.* I thought all along I had believed it: but not until that moment did I feel sure about it."[1]

Some of us, too, perhaps, have need to break through into discovery concerning the fact of Jesus' Resurrection and the fact of His living presence. Too often these appear to us only as another doctrine which is, no doubt, very true and very proper, but has little relevance for actual life. We do not doubt it, but neither do we doubt that the earth moves round the sun, and the one belief makes about as much difference as the other to the way we live our lives. Yet Christ is, in fact, as really alive to-day as are we ourselves.

No more astonishing message has ever reached the world's ears than the affirmation that Jesus was risen and alive. It is no less astonishing

[1] *R. W. Dale of Birmingham*, by A. W. W. Dale; p. 642.

to-day than when the news first broke. But we ought to be living our lives as men who know that it is really true. For so it is. The Lord is risen indeed.